CLEAR AIR

JOSEPH DUVERNAY

CLEAR AIR:
Greater Than Or Equal To One

POETRY

Library of Congress Control Number: 2025903424
ISBN HARDCOVER Number 979-8-9852907-2-1

© JMD

Joseph Duvernay, Publisher
Frazier Park, CA

≥ 1 Maker/Evolution/Nature

≥ 1 Body/Mind/Spirit(Animating Principle)

≥ 1 Theorized Luca/most of Life as men know it

≥ 1 the 'empty' space in atoms/the emptiness of space

≥ 1 the entanglement of all/the web/the knowing/the intuition

≥ 1 Hydrogen, the first element w/out which ??

≥ 1 statement covers the whole of natural numbers

Who knows not the heart of words
cannot know the heart of man.
                              Confucius

INTRODUCTION

First, admission. I cannot remember a time when I was comfortable being told what to do. Ever did I balk, and ever did I do whatever it was, my way – a little or a lot – whatever circumstance would allow. This meant my obstinance would often need to be camouflaged as a mostly compliance with what authority was attempting influence.

I tell this to precursor my 'old ways' years of immersion in the Life of Mind, pursued in prior years, but adamantly in the twenty-plus after retirement from Industry, in which I vowed to write, write, write, which I was given by the grace of the Maker and Universe to do.

As a matter of course there was reading that my working world's twelve hour work days would hardy permit that needed catching up on, so I also read widely, which reading, is the maker of good writing; so many have done so much before. Thereby, I was not interested in, nor did very much, look for assistance not found in the mostly Original texts of writers; from whom – what an education!

In keeping with the above sentiment. For me, that someone outside the self should edit the work was always a wrongheaded idea that I didn't see could be applied to efforts in poetry or philosophy, both arts trying to convey a mind behind the work – at least that is what keeps me reading – an ideas worker. Even though rightly poetry is more in the realms of art and allowed its flights to questionable locals of mind than perhaps philosophy, I concede nothing that leaves philosophy out of that cosmos.

And that leads me to the infamous 'workshop' where, as with most of man's civic doings in the world, publishing weightily included, it is influence – who one knows or has pleased in some way that bugle the day. And advertising, though I succumbed some, played in the world like a bully, so I generally wanted none.

And so, if one is left out, unknown, and off lists, it is one's own doing and a set of decisions to live with (did I hear the pucker of sour grapes there?); which more and more I do with a calm equanimity, furnished by the work – being untiring effort.

Last going, I see this book as companion piece to 'TWELVE AMERICAN DANCES' (2023) which covers roughly the first ten-plus years of my hoped un-interrupted devotions to Mind, with this text revealing the later ten-plus years. I can tell the reader that that twenty years, looking back now from here, went as though it was skis-strapped on a slope . But isn't that repeatedly the way it is for nearly everyone?

CONTENTS

THREE

FOUR

ONE

THE EARLY YEARS

Is it you Euphoria, allowed in new love days?
On the horse and mule trails we met,
packing guts tight; or was it an advanced course of study
far up distant blue risers where
love was imagined when heads would not turn;
eyes fixed admire and neither strayed nor blinked?
 Was it smiles, from concern, that came rush?

Then calls and visits were sweet the new days,
and with the world's best occasions – finding some.
I held up that world for your passing
 and it weighed none.

You were so kind I almost lost touch
with the walking ground and lighter things,
 and of you nearly only thought.

Was it Happiness that ventured beyond, if there lives such;
an escape close of purpose, a ditty land lock;
you in the morning, one shirt blocked
so you could have my scent through your day;
 and the moving world that moved to obey?

'A LITTLE NIGHT MUSing' (FOUR DREAMS ACURATELY RECORDED)

> They hated him yet the more for his dreams, and for his words. - Gen. 37:8
> Show me the dream, and the interpretation thereof. Nebuchadnezzar. - Dan. 2:6
> All the things one has forgotten scream for help in dreams. Elias Canetti
> People do not dream, they are dreamt. We undergo our dreams. Carl Jung
> If a little dreaming is dangerous, the cure for it is not to dream less but
> to dream more, to dream all the time. Marcel Proust

First

Wood embrace of two perfect branches, I'm in my bag, in the pine
snug and safe at the dogleg in the road leading to the house.
Part: my waking trail; and Like in most phantasia, why this is happening moves off,
but I can see sly moon's bright face, and comfort covers again.

Next. In coveralls Dad runs into his garage, slams the door; late evening?
I follow, he complains he can't hear himself hammer,
shows something of a rolling tool case he's modified with holes for what?
I'm floating backward and acceding pleasure at what he's accomplished.
But for the not hearing, it's evident he blames Who, What made/makes all,
the universe, older age. Then, jumping from door to lower level
so spry and youthful, I wonder could the not hearing be so bad;
  then, for a carpenter, it might (be).

Second

Some kind of reclining, hungry. At last,
someone was showing someone a peel-pack of biscuits
and I couldn't wait to taste em! Then, not much.

Third

A cop going between houses very fast on a scruff dirt bike crosses the street
and flies from front to back yard again and again.
Then: to arrest me, but turns into a woman who starts to shrink;
and mother, though looking out of the kitchen window, can't help.   3

I don't seem to need her help, because the woman shrinking can't hold me.
Relief flush! Fast on, I'm running away with something and find my old work site,
a very large building complex in the telecommunications industry;
and I'm in a stairwell, still running; I'm on the mezzanine level now
with the maul able elevator mechanisms and other machinery
that will dupe in misstep.

Suddenly, metal stairs that are but iron railings I'm on there.
Now some hallway; a fellow worker coming through a door
... a job he's in-charging, and bandages dress his hands
from sewing the huge 750 power cables; hat low over shaded eyes;
bandages about the head too.
I ask if he understands there's life after this,
and suggest, 'you can't hurt yourself like that'.
Several pretty operator girls pass, and we break;
 he's going to wash for lunch.

Now, three cars full of people. We're at a country property
and finished some business, I follow the first car through the last gate.
We've gone too far down the road and away from the gate for me to see
that it is closed, so, I'm backing up hard and fast with the dust.
But somehow, I've missed my turn and see all
standing `round a water tank looking up not moving.
Now it's an industrial property I'm on, a bleak campus,
and I'm out of the car, standing off the road on a patch of green.

In quick: soldiers are marching; circa Revolutionary War.
Resistance peaked, I lay down whatever I'm carrying.
The troop form a line and come marching toward.
A fog has followed, and they can't see, nor can I.
As they close, bayonet's hungry, I lay down with hands over head;
they will run me through and over!   But don't.

They pass looking forward, I don't move.

They're coming back but not for me, so, I get up and the fog clears.

As I look left there's a large bay animal on his back like a dog,

it's a horse, hooves in laughing air;

three people are playing with her, I think they're women,

but as they rise and pass, I, `Excuse me girls...'

No! they aren't girls and won't be called that!

But trying to ask for a way out, they pay no attention.

Fourth

Several instances of villainy. In each I wanted out is import.

The first: vague. Second: after noting I was somehow with a poet

I seemed to know, the gender changed. But in euphor I:

"I used your name today." - Pride flush and glad to spread the joy,

show liking, respect for effort - things poetic matter not provenance

(and F you Larkin, I'll *be* an understrappling for naming and quoting,

because those processes by writers read, opened so many doors

to other writers for me, it would be a travesty to deny possible readers,

here, same!) And as poets need, generally, all and any help forthcoming,

mark with what villainy I seemed part of a bad crowd breaking-in

on a group of people in a house; and if not the leader I was mean

in false face-protect and useless stay alive garnered by those useless,

gaming, lured by quick wealth, stealth immorality, as allude, but who,

in my heart, wanted none of, sorting for an out for myself and captives.

 And let that be wish. Struggle for good only!

 While evil, vain, continues. Or not!

WILLIAM COWPER

Love the man! Soft of Heart of so many like.

Soft spirit which soft is poet!

BOOTED AND SPURRED

Nothing to be done. Flashes of lightening, peals of hunger;
(un)wieldy bursts on perspective lift in chairs, go tilt about.
`Use-full-ness must defend little!' someone.
And a breath of eyes-wide soils cloth.
    `Along the less savory, just the facts and close obligation'
you're with Rabelais's Q. booted and spurred ...say what?
`till, in a round with gas bag, you're St. Francis body as ass modifier,
meads and pokes fun at!
    Sharp turn! and days measured in pick-a-lip,
when anxious urged wife and daughters with everyone else to pull against.
It sat, sitting in close relief, the fact, that, no question,
        I was wrong! and apologize!
    There "'ling-broth", heather cod, cheese meat, lettuce
mustard with "antifortunal" rack riding stuff.
So soft bells softer sing unsung! No tool's falderal.'
    As like Good Francis, wary, less sculpts kneaded, find enjoyment
working the `Work, do what can, give what have', healer on!' stuff.
    And Petition, drop hammer to finish grueling days with,
anoint cipher that faint merryweather has music toneday,
does chirp from the trees, as late show reads age,
and you and near-enemy have gone to sea on the net.
        So like des Entoumeures, you've been dysfunctional!

    Notes: Quotes: Henry James; Charlotte Bronte; Abraham Lincoln.
The Friars of the Island of Sandals, and how Pantagruel's Bravest companion Friar
John des Entoumeures was disconcerted; Rabelais, Book V; Chap. XXVII P.595-599
my copy.

COPYRIGHT OPTICS

Would on-line you something
from the real Hosts' dinner party
that got just barely evening started.
Would control what struck spittle at.
 Had in mind so profound a landing
 around globe spun a few,
though on wee stretch of stone & dirt mend now.

 Purpose - burlesque sometimes in gloam,
  much assured by clothes trim and fit,
  accept of obeisance, copied - might barrier coughs'
  phlegm indifferent that beat curry and
  slack slurry any carrier wit of computer assists:
  'there's little to see here,' Copyright Office glides.
  While with humane mind mushin', recursive,
  not independent of memory embed, but also not
  akin those opposite, in late Deep comeuppance,
  'I can't make money if I have to pay for content!' You
  for human understanding scratch and post some anyway.

COURAGE

Find you in front when they look.
Teeth, nail, bone in barrier's wash, but still.
Will notice strain, strength, Licensed-Peace share –
red, green, or black rather than bite -
some prayer-call answered to address as penitent nice.

Matter smattered slim, scratches training
among soldiers' indefensible orders crossed;
      one is a man before a soldier.
Thatch as sea jolts, crabbin' flash a-jostlin' waves
that break the matter of fact.   And a caboose along its hind,
bidden on land, beats its own engine back: that's California!
      Base *and* dance, pirouette; impossible task.

      Someway though Fran, when leaves are abandoning,
and ground sighs cold slate of winter,
in that near impossible, from whack journey
a Job, prodigal, advisedly to a crooked town comes;
settles adversity, sharpens DEI; whom, placed two steps behind
by whom now deny; deserve their fairness deservable,
for valour's calibrate buy.
 At last, by grace of The Allmight, in this, as secretary of allusion;
of sore mouth to plight of keeping shattered, chattering
coward teeth tight in the maul having joined there, you might write.

DICHTER

Straddle gray of shuttle day
and hearthsome oak twirl light off varying baton.
Electric sun, chased up ridge, then the last tree, finally gives up.

Somber stands worder's independence
from various worders edict, cheap confetti tossed de capo air.
Night prowls and tramps lonely measure.
The toothed howl and growl spies of Cerberus extend.

But a speechless rave smiles ritual silent,
and any truck those jack-leg alarums unequip against spite.
Call it: making a wrought philosopher drop his drink.

Then, work-a-slay world without fear bares its falsies.
Settled loam pride belies.
None expect dominance to linger in the raised finger, chaffed spirit.

But histories' hands extend a bathe and a baste
that into non-blink sun bounds.
That could, would, rail, prepared dissections of parts to wholes.
For ease of refraction!

Finally, anyway optioned, with an audience if there's one;
a smooth touch wants a bristle one, rhodomontade with elision;
fascination boat the immerse, and something, if but a word, learned.

Notes: Dichter: [G.] writer, poet. Rhodomantade: bragging speech. Elision: omission. De capo [It.]: from the beginning.

- DECIDING –

Completely worth the cost!
Sit with colors and shades of sky, penseur.
Share with all, not just near imaginary
World-family and Muses by.

Land deep of knee and keep all.
Enough youth may be left to scatter seed with slip scorn.
Thinking long and hard, bite now down on cold's group-tragic
having lived good-turn overjoy that loves more its magic.

Think, thank! what must, Live with trust!
    Shield dread hand, said and acted on!
Argument of life, with big love on the inside pry,
 as attendant worlds dine out on.

Attentioned then, back straight, where sordid leaders meal -
Do you not linger!   Notice when Wind satisfies,
and intelligences' staunch stubborn not new intelligences,
said again. Then about, remember what your Ma and Pa did
as sin swept in.
    And good hearts go with ya!

- FEELING AND THINKING –

Wiley Rosemary, because she is that, overhangs,
grown wild about her Rose; thorny bush of beauty,
dapple petals, rich embroider, enclose we.
These and their neighbors in the garden:
baby Pine, Succulent, and weeds careening in-subordance;
simply charge, especially when freshly painted with waters,
that a sometime senseless, senses commanding human,
appreciate with smiles' shows inward or outbound
as Ahhhs! suggest from lips to the much waiting air;
that which lately hurricane reaches `round to count,
and post recants of what feeling thought.

Yet, you sought the too-many-variables hurdle of dreams
that at times, emotions cannot plead for, cannot find,
that are the sunshine denied, as cogitate lights its candle,
genuflects on holy dirt, and spills a kind of fire over scenes
that might otherwise stand trial for, sit and feel.
 O tentative! the ascent of in-seeing
 relies on and much more sensation follows.

SURRENDER IN HIS GINGHAM HIGH

Art and travel, one wants to tell, and hopes for that.
So drummed gurgle, legs willow,
over felt model green, on ride module -
Who won't tell the truth, have not grown!

Accrual reminiscences spin.
Fighter, forward condescension!
Supple, quiet, had bites on civility;
for diet, for gumbo of pepper, salt initiatives.

And on the other hand, one worder,
by vaporous concentration their graphic,
goat-herding heart's glass, mind's acrostic,
gets like a dog for his chevy's sound on familiar pavement;
the renewed reward without which, no chin to paw or settling sun:
one sentence, the day's stretch, surprised-on at a time.

On yet another, it is as racer the foe (still like and kind).
Doors buffet stays to jim,
perfection sniggles goodbye,
windshield holding aegis-like,
Being surrenders in gingham high.

Record shows the tragic consequence
of fleet, as on a string, chases.
Model he of sobriety parked.
Adult wounds of play life away aside,
owe allowance careening starts.

Seat then, a Charlie scan a map for Kodak's look back;
steely eye done-with. Seven day's march,
and trust from a hundred hidden valleys

behind a hundred massive mountains; summer fires;

L.A. to Fairbanks, the vaca, work hard in situ!

via a once hawg ride – it was I Denali or bust!

Notes: Gingham: (stripped cloth) a clothing fabric usu. of yarn-dyed cotton in plain weave; the truth...a truth, your, their, his, her truth, yesterday's truth. Acrostic: (riddle), cipher, anagram, monogram, etc.

BROTHER NEPHEW & DENALI

Protection through victory, you victor me brother
and nephew, in countless ways
and are like the very days appreciated having lived with.

Men may find referenced – calcitrant – in the journals;
the times strong demanding, content
to establish bred self, to be present in Mother Nature;
slow way round;
                        seeking deep-heart's gallant input

I went up that rocky road to see you Denali.
And the bloody flight of gravel, speed of big rigs, cold,
sore in saddle, nor general travelers' trouble laid halt on.

A sight well the sight benefice of; where standing
adamant the clouds draw away, your height was
three times further up than clouded supposing;
        well worth the ride.

Then to home mountains, where gray now,
remembering the muscle of your height,
with looks on near jagged Whitney,
enjoying still the remembrance - your line of sight.

SELF-INFLICTED

Above the furnished earth, cloud cloister marches, a late patch.
I fold, take cue from tufts of grass who furl nearby.

The jets have wake vectors and disease perpendiculars, some say,
draw down as if blindfold blinds or to foretell cold speed's annulment.

Blown wind works against the seam and tears the bank. I think again:
where have I shouldered brunt so members seat? Do something good for them?

Winged friends in acrobatic feints attention. What is a nest?
'We must accept the effort as heroic that got life here and never dismiss it.'

Combust cars below dirt our paradise, and a road and that patch of sky spell,
spoiled, the wager lives took, which insists it's longer owed: our dry gulch of us.

SLOW WALTZ

Spends time looking for prizes.
No warden, a Lancelot if posy.
  In the sorting forward,
  a failed Parnassian.
Hermetic does not fit like a shoulder socket.
Knees very crossed. While.

PERSPECT

When Mind opened before blank page
cast as greater than she/he in It, chest churned to liquid.
Nodded coward, Self saw, led and lodged complaint.
Citizen Worry! bait the packaged crap's compile!

Pardon chased Homie Over and there were eats at that raillery!
Coffee teemed to tip and sketch an active morning.
Careful! lost step for a favor! Warren habits finally bedded down.
 In the dirt-dust trail over, there's a guy standing!
No! It's that window, on that wall, with treed skip of branch.
And trail's southwest of that!
 The late winter early spring grass seemed crabin,'
`till no! Last late rain did glow sight rich green water gave.
Now brown shows crown all wear underneath!

 On paper, un-Joyeux bordel a merry mess, and if allowed,
manifest ancient Worn as mantel-next somehow.
'Love, most Venerable of all the gods, don't subdue the mind,'
grieving ample Body and Soul, behind, till wails no more!
  Who did the dirt? Emptied what Lasts, Inside,
  to repeated runs up run-less ridges for a token or a high?
  Wrote risk and ruin till high no more?
 Man! Said one 'bold-and-living fire.' And, all The Great Simple Philosophies
 equal The Avoidance Of Ills.
But How to do it?! Implement survives by for and to the crowd
in The Hoped Long Ahead 'Reflected Feeling' Mean Time!?

   Notes: Quotes – Hesiod, Friedrich Schiller.

THE KING

Care along such whither
whether jump and go are worn;
all in ear cry poor the favor
soles weren't better born.

Some were right, some plain wrong,
some stalked their pride within.
Tide matter set to verse was sung,
that some might wash the sin.

But, as in times full hazard,
action speaks but turns quite thin;
sunshine their haze lit standard.
The whole took course the dim.

Still from active, wishful minds,
some plied duty to sustain;
judicious effort crowned the times,
making King Air king again.

- LAST STEM CELL STRAW –

Create one of us
to use, then discard?
I daren't even think it!

ARISTOTLE TO ALEXANDER

"Alexander the Great inquired of his master/teacher Aristotle
what would profit himself, and at the same time
be serviceable to others. Aristotle is said to have answered:
"My son hear with attention, and if you retain my counsel,
you will arrive at the greatest honours.
   Firstly, that you do not overcharge the balance.
   Secondly, that you do not feed a fire with the sword.
   Thirdly, gird not at the crown;
   nor, Fourthly, eat the heart of a little bird.
   Fifthly, when you have once commenced a proper undertaking,
    never turn from it.
Sixthly, walk not in the high-road;
and Seventhly, do not allow a prating swallow
   to possess your eaves.""
       τό γνώθι σεαυτόν –Know thyself
        nosce te ipsum – Know thyself

IT'S AN OLD WORLD NOW

Conceits' chance, gloom vogue, mood match,
gray soaks batch of blister day.
Topples night that moon, its hitch.
Rich her trail; we'll take brighter travels with!

It'll be a window we'll sit by. There'll be ford
of riverless minds, comes across and bridge of complaint.
Our whines Locke the similitude of Things.
Berkley's nothing without a mind to perceive we'll in cue

with dark-continent-taught Ptolemy, Picasso whomever who,
add a Dickinson, a Darger, a Bäker, a Du... Who?

Then, Socratics machine tagged memory,
honest groom knowledge, task-king certain achieves,
while gallop geeks' bombs in rings burst round real –
those civilly challenged who pluck all the good up, out.

But we enlist passion Starter! We'll It when 'mote or beam'
trends in choices, Tunes aura incase that approach in shifts
to segregate. Bone groan sin; torrid tendence, tumbling
to convince starts too! But the rogue killer of man here,
has all the boost snapped out of him.

Notes: Henry Darger: Janitor, Author, Painter, etc. Ulrich Bäker: Swiss-German author.

PARABLE AND PARADOX

Between bramble and edge, you thought yourself out of sight,
as Wisdom - Understanding's sister, 'all awfuls are above and behind!'
came crinkling along on plinthian leg, some road you were on.

Scared plenty, you felt you heard the blue sky, 'As much as any,
darkling beetle is philosopher!' august. After that, consulted sine die excuses,
masticated tramples on intellect and tried outpace to pursue.

Droplets somehow spoke: 'We're after euphemistic serotonin,
antecedent jumble, and know dripper: the well-being's recombinant,
drug resistant, flows; and well we like that display!'

How are wisdom, the ether and droplets speaking?
How pose sets of questions, the answers to seeming closer than ever?
- With no time to linger, lure theory: half in, half out of uniform,

as on the evening floor with the dog, continuing its plum of insight
you native, follow the stream of pure consciousness, where were best,
a long night suffer, 'Per vias recti', feed and Iliad sing.

Because no matter, nor worse, knowledge slurps his plenteous 'wine-dark sea;'
and each hour parable and paradox hither and collaborate;
and with every mind the world is new.

Nor forget 'you are your own ancestor' as Junot to Napoleon.
- Language may stupefy, the desert be bleak, some slip of cognance might,
but lessoned, no more duck and cede. Dig in and write.

PICTURED IN PARIS

Towered the tower;
Vanity praying in time
as close as summed come
captured under track this sun
of several passing centuries together and at one
simple entrance to the coup slide end of things
when Time the optionor takes rolls
and with glum accounts and faded mirror
coffees' the café, inspiration nearer
any city might argue points with
of pros, con, plusses and
plumbed negative's feedy reach
in less moral wages of fancy's deliverance
where Choice allows jump
or stay solid surface
and institutes grace on brief behalf
 to the many times graceless whims of man.

PLAY - PART TWO

Alcaeus: I have an elegy to spin.
          It wants lining and round about
the turf those jazz-men left and leave
trails of smoke inch along society's pages;
I sheath in cloak of non-dress – all Californian!

Sappho: I've my own funerals, and wine
          meets song a while, often,
          as thou weren't killed by God's
right hand much as the left that extinguishes
husks from corm I'll this evening sing and
eat through my lyric that costs!

Socrates: Enough prattle republicans!
          Agree, we are glad sun traverses sky.

Sappho: Yes!
Alcaeus: Why Yes!

Socrates: Then with stela away, in the day's too short,
          Why not pile own ballast! Sift in open mates
          like the barrel chief, and war-dread hatch
as new peace-need to rub raw,
staying tied-down burdened, as we dance in place?
That now, from haunting releases, as mere men
we, as from great heights, say yes Birth!

SELF SACRIFICE

Dedication: French Via the English

I may not match your sound,

how music bounds tight lips,

but I can read the signs saying

ever indulge over living, squeeze

what wants spaces, too far not ripe on page:

        to mort, to mire properly

        so with the near required time

        mopes are born on capacity's wanderings

        every second eve from start.

Moon an inch in the sky

is a way to gray everything.

Each, seldom in the same saloon

passes fastest:

red-away and time speed!

Insights from relatives thought

weren't solving persist; too fast Jimi!

And wandering among Wystan's alcaics,

sad how sinking everything not tied down is.

Notes: Alcaic strophe, after Alcaeus; [Gk Poet 620 – 580B.C. – A four-line stanza.

- TALIESIN –

Old soul, saint of men. In Welsh-land, and bard too.
Count with Aneurin before Merlin.
Say - a gift of God to help a father, aide a son.
Say ultimate catch of the weir, and 'Behold a radiant brow,'
  call him Taliesin!

If sung song sings tale and thinking therein,
it bids welcome how by meditation things were known
                              and vow
the way overflow of myth can junk attribution...
but a poet is always floating on his rough sea of cloud.

So, Owain, Kynon and Kay sing,
Arthur Knights with others round
and picture for us a youth over-wise, a seer,
bringer of fortune, and import your buckets of fish
where no kingly favors sought.
In the shadows, waiting to be called;
relief and honor charge, as sorely put upon.

Chief bard, son of stars, liver of lives;
whom none would strive verse against,
who contended with men; only thirteen when
withstood the eyes and hands,
nearly doubling destruction down
as through time others like, in baskets on rivers,
brought from holes in the ground were found.

So a God-gift, prophet be.
Treemember of the wild.
And the mild wish of whisk wind exalts.
Its Happy, incensed   23

by the fear that drives little men's lives.
  Right with good's might being. But only if you'll do that!

      - THE OLD TREE KILLER –

Oh Yeah! Had his fear on full
of sweat, stinking as the eld wood fell.
Let the old tree killer
do what most the old whale killers have,
find another product.
Stupid plucker! Life sucker! ≤1!
Can't take down any more the old ones!
 Perhaps Eco-tourism for you too.
  Fire-starter, we'll till you!

      WHERE SAT THE WHOLE OF RENOWN

Should we ours, we are burning
Count smirk of bend and blend at build,
raze worthy walls of myth and fact
themselves wend, men, who are yet not enough again?

O Ramses Miamun, thanks for pnt.Awr.t
 lent write that willingness in stone.
Oh nurtureland, lauds for Aesop his mirrors.
O Alexandria, be orbicular in the Bible
so with Cleopatra there rear no want.
O wearied step, soft and fair with Rabelais,
like Heracles at Ceyex "Of their own selves
the good make for the feasts of the good," and   24

no even one tip to Timon or Diogenes of the barrel,

for what was `peanized, made mock christian-like?
oh! the "pagan" monuments, Vasari, destroying!?
Oh dismissed historian boot and throat full-note,
Sphinx faces that would not do? The scathe,
epigrammatic shame that O! It was not them?
who love alepou and troll of fictions evil to say,
deception made gift ready pedigree.?

Here again, Bible aims, hits, splendorizes
treads lost-time front, behind.
Sirach – sorry for some - alone is plenty
to go Azymite or Pro-zymite resplendent in extant glow;
through enlightenments men glass where sat the whole of renown.
'One never put to the proof knows little.'
'No creature is greedier than the eye.'
not for myself have I toiled, but for every seeker after wisdom.'
- like Aesops's tortoise to Zeus, Sirach extends the same gland,
'Better a poor man's fare under the shadows of one's own roof
than sumptuous banquets among strangers.'
'A man's conscience can tell him his situation
better than seven watchmen in a lofty tower.'
- a better Pergamus Aeneas!?
'A man may be wise and benefit many, yet be of no use to himself.'
   Here again Timon?
Quoth the durant sane, humanity is sow!

Notes: Heracles at Ceyex('s): Hesiod. Hecatomb: sacrifice. Timon, misanthrope. Vasari's Lives, 1st preface. Alepou: fox. Durant: of durance. Troll: speak rapidly. Azymite or: re: the wafer at religious service.

VERNAL EQUINOX

Power outage checks. In the moment, on the strafe,
  give what just went... Make no excuse before the verge!
Then thank Reckless, no nuclear winter!?

  Snowing so on poor mountain, flakes loiter over village a curse,
  surrounding land has left by espial, brave trees, arms full,
cry help with load; and crows that waited hours
for moored maelstrom to get over it, are out by the south door quite as fast
as pinions will take in the van.   But see, as flightless man,
I can either hike or sit tight as Fukushima curdles benight.
Wrapped, a piglet these blanket, what wonder then, vernal, that achrastic,
gave-up polemos to cold mischief; and hums brumal, despotic?
 I would cry, but I'm sure it would engulf me.

Notes: Achrastic: after Xenophon's αχρασίς, used (he says by Socrates) in his
Conversations of Socrates pp. 12, 64; meaning weakness of Will. Probably from χρή – need,
necessity, destiny, due, duty, obligation, must, compelled, etc. "α" being "not", etc.
Polemos: [Gk.] war. Brumal: of, pertaining to winter, etc.

THE WORK: NEW YEARS

Over the years in retreat, retirement from the one,
to dauntless, total immerse in other work done, doing,
when a twelve year every-day run at – years to make up, thought –
nursed unrehearsed poems in threes and fives, after the telecommunications,
that came like birds to a sleeping dog's bowl. And found then many by quantity,
and some quality, glanced-on.
Self-possession and questioning, a revamp of process some years consulted;
designated 'rest' in tremble over our now Mondays, Tuesdays and lone Saturdays'
where break, reprieve from four day a week art-fired-on schedule
that's lasted some six or so years at this write, further shall?

It's where the hard, concentrated business-end of effort in New Years
is getting on. As direction, action, purpose and practice head down on the slate write.
 So that having run hard at, find, as always in concentrated, judicious attentioning,
Time went at a glancing pace. And Viola! On a non-descript, slow-ish day and hour,
under hoped protect of kind Heaven; as ghostly apprehension, from the floor or below,
a side, above, upheaves, sneak in. And shows just what Einstein imagined –
your long, short, far, near and not so fast as it headlongs what you and Time have do
through the bind.

Then maybe for a quarter-note you were proud.
And the self-esteem humbled, and abled to break ego from
how, where and when ago.
That maybe lit such paths as - fresh, new - before and a-Stroud,
head still down, in moves on, to tell the world that!
Anyway, reality came to remind of your saying, some ten or so before
'...and Saturday never comes,' with the gasp-wrenched thought
"this is your first Saturday in seventeen years!"
And it was, of rest. And a corner was met at eye level.
And the whole-being reminisce and jolt passage,
cold-pressed, recalled top years, but not just that.
Brought Mom, loving in her kitchen. As Dad and me in our mid-day,   27

Western-movie Saturdays' relished, beneath Mom's brief weekly tallies,
"let them rest!" protective. That was its own goodly poem.
As life, familiar in webs and grown-over old roads through old forests took.
And the joy and pain that is the full stuff of solutions,
with the dilemma of work improved by dreams, on its slide down-chair,
found itself, by that slip buoyed, and chose the closed eye as tutor's care.

This new year, only our second new piece thus far,
from the ninety to one hundred we would have had in years back then,
in its plastic paucity, with stuttered step weighs in, and is this!
Which allows a why and because – on the many previous unpublished,
rewrites quicken and by new-vantage beckoned, one finds
one may indeed have, at heck-pace worked.
  The new making less noise in old's chatterpieces.
  And old and new, both needing, clamber together, lean on and lean back.
   With significantly – much to do yet.

03/23/23 OR THE ON OFF

Truly it did go this way.
The screen showing 03/23/2023 another poem
12/12/12 sang to mind, so blurted in
 to be said... I love the people's head.
The High Insolve to get all there, known or not.
  Where? Well, how could I know, mind?
It's the going, heedless of year!

Or surely not! Though that not, contemplates - are you sure not?
  And Life spun a way on Her lifelike loom while they bustled.
They wonder of profound, and wander wherever Her lands be!
  Good Practitioner Please, your even among,
occasionally will help; even dash in to say a thing
 so marry with beware and forward well.

Then, examined man looked,
but there were few safe places for correct in that burn age,
that business got away with, under sleeve.
Enquire honestly? Look, see little!
There prongs and prods, then, just kidding! propelled
 aware averse; which is the on off!

So, have it. The on off, late inverse in tired loop,
some actions prompt to stop, warning in its way.
        There, shakes hands with limb, Wind, old friend
        who alltimes holds in trance, partner his dance
         of pirouette leaf and bob branch.

Fearless ardent whose omen swim the medium,

T   agent-by-careless, where one crow points,

A   the other guards her six; hail regardant!

L

K   Bring-captor, you are one begin and end of fear;

      and strange to mark your savage start

T   from the same smart art begins with.

O

      The expectant, timid, foundering on rocks, urgent,

T   dare me from my lark, having taken little notice

H   of the sparrow-eating serpent, respect-less.

E

      But 'Sparrows too have a heart.'

      The sovereignty of nations is a heart. As to war:

W   the loss of containment, under-thought, is a thought, but a bad one.

I

N   So, for a while, go past, too big to curtail,

D   whose broad-file piles wore the home for nails

      that mars green hills, coffins with.

Then like mighty wallflower break through brick,

shy-bred Justice wails for telling empire "No more!"

its fan fab tales.

Act the tray no longer empty on its sill;

abide guilt tug its trixy wagon along, be

there love for hug stride right.

And the wayward arm, its wayward harms,

wave through an end.

And oh wind

Primer that primes!

bash men not on foam-dashed rocks!

Admit births in safe, dry ports.

Beneath the cliffs, fair endeavour,
go just that one-better
than beat and bust and bluster clever.

Notes: Shakespeare: "Fools that for a trixy word, defy the matter." "The Merchant of Venice" !??? Argent: silver(y); white. Calchas: Reader of sign, Bird watcher of the Greeks, who sacrificed at Aulis before the setting out for Troy.

THINKING OF BORGES, THEN POUND

Villon, Rabelais, Rousseau, Joyce, Ezra Pounded Eliot
entangled better than reportage clever sans learning like!
with its life of privilege; take a wish and on others dump.
   A man's debt to base-safety of others in society, never cashed,
un-dischargeable, until death, like it or not pulses on.
And no ant even has done less her habit since time rose.

   Nor do we allow dead-blast human language to say other!
Ant must in her own, 'Cause everything thinks it's human…
the center of the universe; center of all it sees looking out.'
as Bro Watts roughly, in simple reportage this
other end - of feelings' observational hearts-ish pumped.

   Good Maker, his clay naming privileges gave, not to add perplexities.
How since? To see what things are, and offer best of own age;
answering Incoming felt-measure, Intuition, which all species, ala themselves,
and Poetries that ever lurk, mark are the good writings'
which are so often a courage for courages' sake!   So 'Lay seriously!'

Without which, excuse of ignorance smart on wilt tongues,   31 conscious in confess, leaves realms un-sought,

realms that entire villages, rummage rubble through, sustenance after.

Tear, at ruffle being left, associate for joy outside; his Huck to that Iliad,

Dune, Gore, Executioner attend, Bertrand Russell point best,

and too, '...to have,' as Mssr. Borges, 'the dream have its way with...

I (like you) don't want to interfere with it!...' and stack that! To start!

Habit, that protein strung to clean, that in barnyard hangs; says

He of himself, this M. Borges, that he had no Greek,

then the 'worker' proceeds citing ancient Homer;

sprightly. One has to clean the meat before can cook and eat.

Send -- at 'they then each;' out of, at every ray, augas, imaginable;

as the math has heir interval; social vector with peace etiquette

and faith in goodness, that goddess is! And with strokes argues

from other planes, that have come, gone, not haven't! inherent and

  so ranges the populae possible! Stern world is daily proof

  of this, and species evident in the look of smiles similar, mirrored,

file: Yes! Scrubbed! And loose conspicuous, wild horse rides!

Fast! --- Calls against bad for good quiet ghosts to come.

And rank higher than bright rhombus that does not sit, floats!

Then, so, October wind with troubles clarify;

and principality of precedence benefits, takes and in naming revels;

quaint happiness, present with books and libraries Pele-ing.

There then, out of all he's drawn, man, finally finds he's drawn himself.

Another silken beam, on a travel air caught, at five-thousand or any height.

And sounds moves may Hollow in the may of dreams that deal wing.

  Ae, gone like a Patroclus in Hero's armour, bethink thyself,

  hedna (bride-price), and a Hector shaving, says, Come to us then

with our fipple in hand, Chi Rho! θοῦροςThouros (rushing);

τρέχωtrechish (run, leap, spring) even. Resplendent, in our armour denied!   32

And Din-following Artemis of the Golden Bow will await in a courtyard.

ἄρήιος Araius ἡγεμόνευε hegemon eunatheisa well-putting-to-intercourse

near the God-let-fall river; ὀρεσίτροφοςorestrophos mountain-nursed;

Dochmos, at slant: pausemenon pausing polemoio war from.

There Archilochus adds - who 'Glaucus, bloom Giant of Leptine.

Most honoured. Eldest speaker;   discovery made of suspicions;

- ...how Glaucus, it is in possibility of going guiltless

Through one hundred seasons of calm as leader/strategist

That explains this kind of having stood with the lot of Poetry.'

And also, 'Universal Love. The name has brought you None

of the breathing gardens of discreet women.' - Here, scrumfull

shoulders SAY, One man come. Him, love be awful man, Tell!

Him say love to die Dem baby lie. Ja know, you try. But dem too awful! Why?

Kill everything to die? Cheek turn kill I? How? In what company,

the doggy or the cow; or mayhap in that graceful of glad Butterfly,

Papillon. The Art of Poetry will be in there jostling how!

Note: Idea from Jorges Borges, Writer of the last century, God Keep! Suggested out of later life, a poet aught not tinker with his/her poem. I say, unless one somehow must, as it seems to call for it!

TO THE END OF ESTRANGEMENT
('EZRA POUND IN LONDON 1908-1920')
'Magistri et ipsi ingenium nostrum fecerunt'

For love's trials, tenzon, 'citadel of worth,' sinew 'rather than surface'
(mind the harp and drum!) Field ploughed; now care of the art; seeds
sown harvest-store applied start. 'A report...;' pen bold, green
in success and fail recruiting head; mockery, curt means its traces here.
'Cum grano' bulwark, some gallery dreams lent, word and phrase
shield writ; 'harder, saner,' following rule ancient, of two, para shoots
want of service; marker of dreams, wand to minds, charges on and off
cheap sheet, groaned over poor trash, tract and spore any short of
purpose, being 'something in it;' by now Whistlers' pard blear walls!

Sidelong scoon, men condense to small, crooked structures;
pressure of 'storms yet to come' whip unknowing; your horses
rear foehns' thrash of huff to top, 'e platz mi!' We sit with our sifts.
By nod, now hubris, crack shell artist – known, sleight hand
of the taker, least part human, bad thought weathering
singe Earth - ring matter stilty jewels `round! Give rubric.
'Oh, easy enough!' Confidence mine; for tune, nourish cries.

Strap oldsong, height-of-discern, astonish, bienvenue and
how'd you do! and act against slouch till evening, settling which
true lies and belongs to whom, alumnus critic. For dearth tithes
and usury shades in the cold of that tower, wooden or not;
cup and dare these eyes sight to glaze; 'sed sum laetus!'

Liberator, image, swirl and that hole - authoritarian, at length,
that breach, that tangle knot, cleanse with nearer wish and prayer;
crime, never eloquent, sue; weighed-pardon calmed return fair,
efficiency mowed. Bring action-the-shotcaller© 'identity of structure'
and love what you have done or hate it, slippery banister and crutch
prone the mid ground. October sings of brotherly love, we page now!

To Pieria who chant, canzon. Where's but careless aside a cart
aride a lane, set to study arise in the angle of loves and philosophic
composed. And was it, is it, all this time, art employing blame?
Took he all his loves for damsels distressed 'herb, flower and root'?
Yes! 'For God Is a good man, Madox, a kind man, good brother...
    and God Is our Father, and God Is our Mother.'

    A 'face like a blessing', some receipt of that Saavedra, to repeat!
    'Short sentences founded on long experience' he.
    Ancestor cred crewed view culled different; and
another Aias throughs a stuffed middle, we pour out a round,
    mind the hyacinth, try to live strong; so that repress,
left no sharp to rounden grinding down girding happiness,
a-crush rescind of evil, rock for sky, all of a piece, is counseled –
as proof to the hard problem of mercy alive in just forgiveness,
    your want then! – to the end of estrangement!

            SMOG
        Dost see boundless sweep of air lappet earth about in yielding arm?
        Hold this to be Zeus and believe it God.   Euripides! Says Cicero

While in court-we swoon brief ladies
spread attire as balloon dress, outmatch
the active men, their hat and ply of rev and tight pant dailies
that must, in vicinity of a 'too snug for us!' catch, be;
of mood and flip impersonations, at fine and happy, impersonators make,
whom themselves gasp fragrance in tear tumbledown
o' lies beautiful; their eyes unfriendly, sun over-rake burnt
of coal in upward sty, that over jeer scars grate. Pause buy.
Others, deep thought reels well above flyers, beefeaters, carers
repair against the others 'will not!' apologize – to its doors,
open somewhat on a let somehow, from the put-upon, solidarity in,   35

as drain with pained rivers, sizzle on mere whiff of dream,
tooly independence, tearious play that apps in the city and lapse on the street;
so drony innocents glowing endless gaols, from Get-a-move-on wardens seem
country club in quartered reams with fascist facets, purged, ae the heat, beat.
    Later, whole erect endangered species, death-trapped gloom
from dead zone own, lift, light lamp to sign that reads: man! Who lassoed noon!

UNDER ONE

Two stones for the lid. Two or three hundred bones under it.
Some smooth, some serrate to ease passage;
for clear's sake, he left by the wheelhouse door.
You can come with your cloak of mannish madness
gore unrest, reddish jacket, that patience will not wait.

Four in the sun bake. Eight by the rear door open hearts' gladness.
Flame of Warmth meet the dove that Love is!
Rotate shepherd, heir to duty and rights higher,
means and cause of heaven, you are who
not lack of desire, nor fists clever negate.

That madness has a captious face. But Worth won its endless race.
Stern under the sign of One, selfish learned it could not
with saint, men and angel, to evil entangle come.
Tomorrow peer, civet now.
Past will sew cloth of madness down!

In kernel inception words to be saved thought thought would too.
That through missed memorization waves accustomed to growth
sin over and their staves, nothing in the secret manner of security keyed safe,
felt sure or over a nigh westering gladness gained.

36

VIGOUR (E=MC^2)

Into her collection of honest, Fashioner.
From! ricky `round, touch in opposites
Burton his ΑΛΕΞΑΝΔΡΩΣ battled.
And good! all wisdoms remain with the people!

They who the Tiger's Tail tread Kurosawa
have shook monk-colds' flagellate,
and blanded, daring now, raising-nuns to apple-gate,
priests from tacky torture taunts, are sneering. Come!

The where you are, these mothers in hollow gear, all,
having beaten trained troop and sports hero to the fight for rights,
for retirement of unsubstantial, unsustain to wear
and from twain scoff us a solo mercenary or gathered might,

that have chartered all Walcotts to Mexico are quite angry.
Each an Angelou in glasses, scarf;
add through chaff, tumult Archilochian; arts shift to prow,
and still, not now first-time firma has wholes to exploit;

and apart, send odious tracker in mouse gear to un-notice
with men, how horizon is making round,
reckless, in-hesitant blow fish - its and more,
that in the mouse's quarters men are to be sound.

Now Dads and Moms, and Larkin's last difficult... etching
narrowed in rows to please seem doing that.
Rose-symmetry cones Pinõn, on bough extremes mount;
only hope, kraterros, under tortrix will surprise, and nock hit at bat.

Yet yew, bronchial corners balling a few, laughs,
how much put-upon Monterey, spiring hers

banana'd up her highest stalks, aloft and abaft,
to escape busy waters, like animal and men
in life-raft prefers getting out.

Crawl then do, the low halls through purple manzanita
only a few forest dwellers know to go back to,
 To deracinate rob talisman its destructus wound, Marietta!
rub grateful eyes over the early spring carpet
where not many with ornith go in lanes through the trees. But would!
 Or racket-adhered Jays with, celebrate some small success.

Notes: ricky: rickety; Ricky Nelson's 1950's and before, untrue world. ΑΛΕΞΑΝΔΡΩΣ –
ALEXANDER, Richard Burton. Flagellate: whip, scourge, etc. Phillip Larkin.

POETRY: VAUDEVILLIAN

How hard Earth your soft look seems part your mystery mastery!
Of E-Prime and its education something may indeed be said;
there the ἐστι (esti) being and οὐκ ἐστι (ouk esti) not-being is Parmenides!
Ἀλλα σύ, (pointing) οὔ τί! But you! Not at all!
So how, Maha-unfinish, display terrors, you, in observants work?

Once, a tome would like to have completed, did.
Now volumes pile hurly and translation of some very aged text
has anxious where sits far-arrayed and dispersed in dolt directions,
time-stamped of bare-and-take-it that efforts every attempt.

See how Natures' wares precious present?
Is in control would have in life? By God's leave, yes!
as with aid and assign-recall fantastic earlier His saying...
'Go down there. The field of Troy, the hurricane wind with tassels
by which eagerly shaking, scatter the heroes Achaeaus...'
as He Zeus Apollo emboldens; as might, as wish,

38

a group some late modern anti-heroes' glitch with.

Observing, meek of miracle, add of what is not us.
Not man! Him? No! he is not The Author.
Though, if can keep the body and save the mind,
health survives better chances. So why not admit Universe?
Give God His Himalayan Eagle's height, California, Condor;
and push, I think, that many simply care for Creation?
It so pleasant simples! - Take less... make less mess.
Not for you, sad police officer, faulty first-responder to no-work
disaster's aspires; again, many arguably own out leaving;
one's government being meant, whom from must amend.
And every citizen ought move to safe future among,
in the being presumed doctor, judge, handyman!

- Huh! don't insult! This is no boot-strap, whom to lower rungs clamour;
that tragedous blight of enslavement - enslaved are enslaved by enslavers.

Conducted you a simple, fact free route at wills' invention over slight
and _ you're or you all are - locked out of truth where the many millions
 of collected works trepid named, move!

Bold cheats, their breath tests, air analysis, convict Them!
Exacerbants, who the rot to life always were -
against resource-poor, their stolen-gains, their bonds tighten!
And wrath, death invites, both mediately and immediately in withdrawn crinkles,
and lowers over, as She Earth from that star scar beckons. And Entropy,
or Heiddy's – 'Sobald jedoch das Dasein so >>existiert<<, daß an ihm schlecthin
Nichts mehr aussteht, dann ist es auch schon in eins damit zum Nict-mehr-da-sein
geworden. But as soon as Dasein 'exists' in such a way
that absolutely nothing more is still outstanding in it,
then it has already for this very reason, no-more-there-Being become.'-
happy, searches forever for fill her larger vacancies. And we? We shall
not arrive thankful mad fabrications sayer! Will not pose bliss in polluted streams,   39

and are-in-mud-stuck trying to get out, to green every human dream.

_____

Instructionary, below, is my belief. Not detail expounded. A paper, such.
But Yo Homey! I'm with ya! So passages in Greek translation follow optative.
And old soldier, poet Archilochus is what, with accord!
As with Jesus, Musashi, imperative, true meaningful arrival bought
and dredged - brought reformed, I now and then
to think the text of modern issue began, a thing the website (Greek)
was 'putting up, ` yet it could certainly, I thought, have come
from ancient logics emotional. Or as said other,
one's acolyte overripe in discovery suspension, to sample and over-invite;
but present with the thicket above reader for your reading sake. So...

EPODE (Archilochus)
Stood in old Greek poetry, the epode or song
that specified exactly three strophes,
ideas or lines of the chorus as its metrical form.

It had characters concluding and tragic reasoning
throughout the whole of the choral dance.
What is the Typical plan?

Thesis or laying-in of the situation; commentaries or
action of the play, and conclusion. Thus, the play itself
unfolds like sheets of lettuce from the place of wiping clean;

(kitchen)(privy) or forgetfulness/unknowing whose foundation
is the philosophy of applied reasoning; stage.
This Archilochus let bloom verily.

Assist in the utmost, these seeings into the consideration
of jests in your presentation, the design purpose of which
is to figure poems, a mine in two-rowed couplets
of strophes or pivot point sentences,   40

ideas producing from splendid, elevated lines of verse to light verse.
These poems themselves, these tellings of epode

blossom from slight story. The very nature of in-putting
these bear me in their chorus-dance poetic of being family with.

Your stories, the best stuff you have, what Archilochus,
of these observations you first made in art are you questioning?
This having stood up; this bravery, this keeping the story straight,
this balanced modeling of meter and seeing-about of thought, feel;
logic as such, verily, is born of the very pointed and so warlike joker lightness.
   (For the reviewer's voice, one need but substitute this first-person narrator
for a third person. In any case, the idea is I think - worthy!) ON ARCHILOCHUS.

NO NOT NONE (OUK) STUCK

Ouk some coverage, till average ensconce
tried-for and the knowledge of elder attachments
terse in plasma, bobbed territory for bubb attacks.
Hume, among phenomena, still percolate thought
and the passions that rule over each, their reason.
We say he means the Heart, κῆρ k(c)aer as 'Omer croons.

 So pleased among the fleety geese, few empiricists that high,
too far the bar, alone, wings lift, fly, land blisses with blesses
and the dense dire miss with rich knowledge, on a day, one exact opposite,
where much was known, of sad dad spectaculars, where yet looks-back piled.
Whence no gain Theodorus, sends Socrates back to sit his haunches.
But sanely with the institutional and corporate insane insuiting,
"never sinking to what is close at hand," finds him, from where his ancients led
off - from proper-prior Africa and the Levant that knitted Greeks,
that knitted Rome. Where later, Wittgenstein knit Russell; Nietzsche, Hegel;
and Aristotle, again going back; not much after Kant, on shelves dusty and dusted,
is still Plato's far from dotard beard platting; as the Black, in latter days
is intentionally left out, by traitors to scholarship, which is Truth out.
- That unto single-use privilege does not now bow, this truth,
sweet blind in attributions' that too, now, are scout the evil,
and harm of those many leavings out; showing, as saying,
    Heidegger this time, clomping along, Husserl under arm,
    respectful of certainties to make sure about.
Those sureties in sheer, that with refresh,
on the un-clot-board of right gleams, flowing south!

There to compete and complete, our bully Bertrand Russell says
and we agree: 'A good world needs knowledge, kindliness and courage.
It does not need a regretful hankering after the past
or a fettering of the free intelligence, by the words uttered long ago
by ignorant men (or less so). It needs a fearless outlook and a free intelligence.   42

It needs hope for the future, not looking back all the time
to a past that is dead, which we trust will be far surpassed by the future
that our intelligence can create... and No human being that I can respect
he goes further, `needs an untruth to sustain him.'
    Add those humanists' words that settle worlds, and saves selves,
the you and I, us, everywhere! that come with and after,
the holy wrap true philosophy is wholly in. And the heavenly attempt
at direction and thrust, even in going passion,
  to lift dan's feet from his stuck circulous.

A SERVICE TO ALL

    Well who gives a flush what he thinks anyway?
And there they were off to a race no man's ever won.
Yet another thought...that's the way it is with, at the troughs of man...
yells Yup! Success! Everyone eye the uptake of pleasures in varied rag!
As from the stores of squirrel, even to the old sculpts, gone now,
of government work... when on the inside... all's gravy! Meal-ticket! -
To a thing of real value always flying fast. To a Service to all!
that buys nothing in the store nor in the special harassment parking lot,
for lives lived backward. Collection being no duty,
but duty a collection of disciplines. Or sense incumbrance
that afar-off laughs. Scratch, sniffs the hearts of thought!
    Yeah, I guess I've too, for honesty, with my Buttinski handy;
tested, corded, in hand, at a main frame of life, did not connect! Alright?
But laid by! And to others gave the given cinch for-self-same-as-for-other(s).
    Saying No! wouldn't want it on my pallet! And Left more man evidemment!
Foolish to argue with a moron! And strayed not far from the fear and fright,
rightly felt for self in much of... what came, roll, over the previous silences
from somewhere. When, in a hurry to face there giant, some, like good Uncle,
mason of free-speech among the royals, Voltaire,   43

for men, gifted as much or more than we know, even who have studied him.
Widely panned irrelevant is now afresh. In your time (Name it not mine!)
flash-the-now-air seems both warrant and sanction.
` Cause, if it's not hate, its hunger, throttles reals in kills!
  As all lace braces for thought on, throughout!

THEY WOULDN'T WANT TO BE YA

Sleep through the baffle? They could have done that.
Or awake, mind, heart, hand and opinion surrender
to get and go long; to line on a stage. "Smile big now!"

 But truths had hitched, panting patiently
for said ride and run or two, to bad water worse water,
bring some meanness to exhaust and thirst, to heel.

'I wouldn't want to be ya!' always parted from
in the face of slack or poor poetry trying so or un-hard.
But they wished the best for.

Still, they wouldn't want to be you! Smiling at nothing,
believing the dollar-eyed editor's clueless accolade –
some wouldn't want to be ya carrying Dame Literature
back to pre-school, and philosophy too.
   Pitch, slope, drop – 'Wouldn't want to be ya!'

TWO

AFTER ABSENCE

It was so much a pleasance
I took it as sign.
We two declared through the later time
would flourish together finally; your spirit, mine.

You fancied your queries,
we sought 'of a feather' agreements.
Fine and respectful waited missives at the start.
While your courage to outreach, was it bereavement's loss?

There personality came, posh, at last to play the lot;
we pushed and shoved to secure our spots
in go gargantuan heave of things.
And the hills we built lost early-laid tops.

So much - sweet, kind smart heart,
feeling more than saying.
Ahoy! Cruel jab splendid out -splay
with cold disappointment on both sides to stay.

To see it now no answer seems;
we had, unrecognized, stepped past at full tilt.
Hot sun remains unchanged; wind travels – what else can it do?
Is this loss of two, destiny, as guides down the chute?

WE'RE HAPPY

I'm here, with her. We're some anywhere, warm and cozy.
Life smiles our turn, we locate great gladness
just where with nearness, one by way of two hit, miss.
Then - much as atom, the universal one is both here and there,
saying of itself, that it is point, and wave that blankets -
the old anxiety I ace, having turned, a moment aside,
her not to find, "I can do friend and artist!" I empower I.
But life coincides, as attention to the one, makes the other stand by;
  and lovers just won't do that.

So gone. Gone in my turning and not finding her,
panic pushes into run, her geography or where to turn I know not.
Questions at unimpressed strangers fly from mouth,
of a way home, a way up and out to districts known, own abode.
Still, relief with exhaustion sits a bulk; and it's true long island,
  I can't breathe, but you know that.

Spurn and bad directions take final toll.
The old broken part in its sure monthly start,
riding, a therapist might say, if I had one,
tells of blame to lift from, or, of a trapped artists' heart,
that will not long stay.   And you wake to absence.

Further, far wide of happy flung, from exhaustion,
the dream tells of what's left undone.
Search and accept play jilted part;
the blame his, not Art's as she whistles, and tries hum!

Foolish, among the bodily soft, breaks many a one. Dear leader,
here is not that attention; but the work, on its proper gladness, drunk.
Which accomplished, Retainers neglect and concentration the watch.

So she eats at her winery and feasts at your troubles' table,

and you wonder why you let her. But foolish is an artist in love with a person.

So much so that among the body soft, ease of proximity,

nostrils filled with ambrosia; the warmth her presence chooses

at each footfall away from her, urges cold to do the torture you crave,

perhaps not owning it, and by these painful mechanisms, you're saved.

So Art, no conciliation, her own entity and excellent in own trickeries,

does and does not, another follow, when in her element.

And that intentional intuitional, firy and difficultly invisible one

senses loss and anger, but is set on her clay, canvas, paper,

and is not of those who at what they've done deserve disfavor,

   for a wonder, an awe she is too, now and later.

So, from one you run, while wishing to come closer,

while the other shows you health from the breathing sun.

Cites huff, anxious, you're lost in. Still, the wakeful relief

and full breathing of workable Good Sense comes.

SOFT MIND
BECOMING ACQUAINTED WITH F. HOLDERLIN

He was called to be mad. Named in stillness
by monied rule of spoil-spread opulence in the over amount;
whom too 'sane' of common average, admitted only curt caning
and swift shuttle aside in otherwise elegant lives.

Meander, notice and care consideration give if once eyed right!
And little scrags foraging fours, near grind carriage wheels,
give truth plenty in case, cause, pause, in sight's boot reveals.

Compare, genuflection, if only slight, skip-scatter- send truncate train
of thought, hold later years as translate, only another way to say a thing;
like Goya's dark, soundless walls; precaution breached much.

The World, good and evil set equal on table-plays of forces,
eagers energies bigger than the wider cordons are blows ripe for.
Where scorn, low of bows and praise of groans within, without
directs man -- erect a crest of mediocrity where most will incline!
brink at feet --- appear ready always, with discuss dither,
to smile, fault, banter fit for forget fever like!

Oh, leaking gas tank nuclear wants its way back, do not allow!
There, to water and air their best insults hove, all mistakes grip bidden.
Landed nonesuch wreaks havoc, where could, would; did we?
when Concise, Humane decisions could have been Made?

Oh jell! Now get gentle the art of ways, ever the work of man to pacify
negotiator with patience, truth. And the Kind in real worlds and real lives
outstretched, far out, sane in the province, a la le 'insane' deals insult.
   There perhaps Feel They (allow) and know, more than not.

BEG OF INTUITION

Well! You can start from mid-air and land nowhere;
walk over um. Wink, non-authentic. Or,
let something between you come.
And take something with you when you go, please!
Use crushed berries of Mistletoe, per Aesop
catch unwary birds, all under the one survival category;
or set some up at one-man celebrations
   for brave women to stand under.

Search for better whys than comrades, loved, dying, without you there;
or fame, honour, the usual like, among them, among men!
that allow the killing of Innocence, that durable adorable
that has many little alters, altars laid for death
to which, the quicksand of man's welcome welters.
 Well, suddenly, a Croesus or an Iago being,
save friendship or let her turn? Whatever do,
Light will increase at inflexion points due to overall collection.
Energy swim, out in, among the empty ware and trance clean air
   bring sane animals to scrappy knees some!

But at crimp, waste wimp on the air, roped, harnessed;
that water pouring in that very little life? In the life of the Galaxy?
Treasonous! You may not!
 And beg of intuition, though she is wary of disturbance,
to finish where for a night lie her many occurrence.
Thereupon, one 19th century French artist exemplar colourist might.
Who, of the ones he encountered speaking, was to Daphne not immune
in her quiet poison, was a lover of Maker of leaves... and we had hopes
of countering dollars' contagion on our wee patch in our day
and hand something sooth in a brown paper Rapper to await universe,
to converse, conserve, welcome, please deservant; illumine
the human condition - Asimov! And in this are paid! Having found something   50

of use in the ruin and finish!

  But the shave-more-than-half-off any endeavor greedy gather.

And treated panic when the big-wigs were in town was no better,

despite all the practice, at making regular employees less nervous.

    In the house and senate Empty was on. We loudened alarum!

    that citizens might rout if not root the liberty abhorrant.

    - Updates may follow!

Note: After being confronted by Apollo otherwise, the story goes, Cupid tells him that he and His bow and arrows are of far greater glory than his (Apollo's) and commences to pierce both Apollo for love and Daphne against. In this, chased by Apollo nevertheless, she begs in prayer for the destruction of that beauty that compels Apollo's ardent, and is turned there and then into a copious laurel with bob head. From then on Apollo's favorite.

ATTENDANCE

They will have to raid all their stores,
call every ledger this or that to verify.
Claw paws through the mess, find the sawsall,
weep Aunt Bess.

Will need weapons. A pack-full uniform of oxygen
to bore through airs' ordered sickness. A book.
Let it be there notice of blankets' excess over the place.
Things, phenomena fasten through full-spectra minutes, ≥ 1.

Last. Will need to use the humanity they hold, of weapon,
however asleep, in whichever depth! to wreck hate with sublime,
so millers' wives old stones, round, roll up; and those
having carpenters as husbands a lot of house on frolic ground raise!

This is the tail of their dragon touched, coup count,
that has Grief, the cheapest thief, aside,
in slowness of catch, full awareness,
the living-steer that reached no influx.

An any, such as might brights of love, solid earth-soldier, back straight,
no part in a blind watch take; more heart
on the pre-bash field with the inserious will have been bet,
nor cast with the snide, aside, so cerulean a bright wet planet.

WITH THE ANIMALS

Yes! One could derail screech of hawk;
follow with eye and arrow.
See into the tree of things,
Get livid with laughing crow.
      Climb the peak, go lark with traitorous dogs' bark.

Along a ridge binge
on the watch of you, town below.
      Some were saying how in themselves
      they were lost, reek in fear.

You must not care in your caring,
but go Epicure's λάθε βιώσας living in hiding,
      from which cowed-alive see you buck then:
      now mother*^*^er, I will track, trace and eat you!

WITH THE ANIMALS II

Let their eyes not want your work,
especially if toward destruction of anyone or thing it leads,
which reads, me thinks, a must be
too much or little in the mean of, that does easily happen.
But also if that bulky set of discredited industries, that unjustly
to their civil destructs, a space is given, have them see
in your eyes, a history not want to eye in their holy shame,
unholy pain of, that you'd no truck with now or later.
       To sell a life for a charm,
          To glass bead upon the arm,
          Is to tyrant in the strict worse sense.
       To fool be of preen, smile, hidden tense.
But If I tell you of all the common man's miseries
distributed by these in bulging buckets of excess,
and of the stingy buckets of their 'best' proportions,
you too would howl long yells at spinescent moon
to little effect, believe me, yes!

PRAYER FOR THE LIVING

It was mother or another forgot, when lowered to kill innocents.
Bad dreams in the carriage 'War is terrorism!'.
Redemption un-fits these!

Tools, tables, graphs; history's heard the words 'We kill to liberate!'
that smarts.   Few lessons recall a kindness; blameless,
unaware, impotent pressure sues.

Across that, a summit topped, calculus vomits; cadavers pack;
hides count, while vile disquiet scarlet paints on lower atmospheres.

   Post, sufficient to indent: what hour muse went
or map of mathematic and science thru which some never would;
tooled for die like Thoas thought of Hector in the wars,

   `This is a marvel my eyes present' - thinking him dead.
`That back again stood up death-avoiding Hector!'
And there's the short of hope prayers will not mend.

For a time, below interest, elsewhere nom'd, there lives no lush part
for them Johns' come-trying and Janes' so fine; named
a bunch `a fu^*ing Does who ingest hate, eject anger.
   But quell me anger now!

WHIRLED

Mystery, the hold reason would not, bred exhaust eyes
squint disaster, at an Inn late, late a night.
Where sat one of waters, cast hair tied ruly scorched mass,
partly hidden, marking in new awe relate –
  A forest of tall ancient, so ready for fog, cloud,
  even skim onslaught, climb vista there your bays high the sea.

  Disembarked, walking in dream those trees, a call from waters,
  I shook out my rock the whole day, cast off sea legs
  and the trends turned. Stubborn hard of dry earth, I'd forgot
  witching-night speeds in woods over arb to lose seen.
  Gut, grieved, conscious, rattled; thirst enjoined, and a coin
  loosed from what I thought were sealed pockets, and I trek made
  out of there so with fine cottonmouths, yae provenance!
  Tome on breeze, wreak denier's haze might
  bid Wind of Change continue evereach, touch of everything.

  Life at sea be's the be all to-the-end of tempests call.
  You'll see, heart through gulp (the self, a knowing does?);
  wave surge rush and flush the gunnels, balls tight a gut.
  And love of calm eternal seas so early in furlough,
  a moment sparked, now only with fade memory can call up,
  were very nearly `till just now complete in loss.

  But I will tell – the sea is not my enemy,
  As the high and lowlands are not yours;
  sylvan shimmery do slide begging in its utmost!

  That – to who whirled, gumped in dream,
  signed the wheel and hologram, so many dial and switches,
  plying their waterships (the which men have long)
  over those mighty wet roads; cast drag their garbage,

56

that no lies about the insanity under consumers' eyes tell –

stiffened in repeats – where shore, the very salt air

with innocent flora & fauna at man's high masts dire warning pipe,

broad in outreach – is that we speak.

I marvel at how I shall go on, where I am from;

plowing the filth men have so very wide, for so very long.

But I will rest now, and back to the depths go when morrow suns.

I doubt I will see you there.

Say, did I skip anything? He questioned, eye rubbed.

No! we all sort of shrugged unknowing, bewildered,

swingbobble heads and signed off to our particular groups and fears

Well – because that's near yeah? But now in decrease not nearly enough...

Just sayin' said sad Oets© in perusal,

sometimes at home in themselves old egg.

"...POET IN SILENCE"

Boldened, oft broken; the far mountains rue eyes rubbed,
scoff cool blue of gentler years. Wearing 'dodges,
vague predicates – transitive closure of binary relations –
the ancestral' as castle; and as after, those near asked
of the foregoing: shout - so unheard voices, crouch brows,
steep climbs, poor old Dionysus in his uh-oh! Circles
misunderstand; with that-maker-of-lays off on his toddle-loos,
whirling in devotions' corners, someone said, Careful
getting drunk with poet, you may not be able to like it!

Softening, ethos, pathos, bathos, logos, with
vanished hours wisp, scaup under; high-wing sharp with air –
his, her `pinion all the once! But no matter: not in book, or
on sheet torqued with pen. Post splot, worked-out
on a country road, that may, the old fabric, have had,
of diverse with its enormous weight to the trouble to add;
so, the worst treatment of '...the poet in silence' --- circumscribed;
said saddest of sads, in their 'department' Le always otherwise
bee in bonnet –   you have the mic and metric!
Something churns in that where! --- not lay fall rights remembered.
Avoidal this tragic dears August in choices. As Mind, Fate helm,
and e`en worn sheets of Wisdom tear, consume, hole, hide
and side in far off days that may never come.

Still... Cognicenti among: words mean, sentences seem.
Paragraph fill; chapters call other chapts to question.
Stanza Monday-modeling, long sought ourselves to counsel with.
And Story told to annotate a draft, blames –
Epic, go out a cut the grass!
 Under strains, Life guides, blinks, we try our best.
 A gasp, gulp or welcome laugh.

Note: "the poet..."- G. Steiner. After Babel ("The Hermeneutic Motion") on Holderlin's Greek translations.

ON HOT PLANETS

Dark cloud, you're in brood from the sea this yarner.
I see you exigent for the moody often inflexible
troublemaker are and ask you allow my obeisance,
for I have no tangle if you'd on!
  Get you to your hierarchies!

Then, balling hail bridals clank and dent of not just hard
but softer surfaces, and ding dongs everywhere.
I said, with circumstances appropriate hail, my faith in thee
is not changed by efficiency, because you know
  the roof over there in our studio leaks!

Only to be planck'd constant that in out-window inspection,
on hot days, on hot planets, in zero-avail conserving,
hail is in too big a hurry to un-hail ways
to pay any solid attention.

A KIND OUT

An American King, of a Bull once,
"He knew a kind of physics, but he didn't know history."
Sensing a policing of Black,
in which pilaster-stance is upon the rick,
taut force blanchness that neither sleeps nor breathes.

You've... their stoop in the field,
on haunches round a light?
Whose eyes will no more of that?

In sky, manumit of weather, spring's seed carpet,
with the skin of matters sources off!
In satchel, you. They in afterlife.
  In this then it was at or about fiftieth you found
Maurice of Africa, Theban legionnaire of Martyr and Spear
chivalric'd in Euro, El Creco modeled too light.
Information could have used as a child, but alright!

Insouce in sam still attempts manning him.
This write goes out tonight!
Rocky firma accesses reciprocation's bites;
relish goes ahead and chews the vacuous, being only right!

Notes: MLK on B. Connors. St. Maurice: noted to have the spear that pierced Jesus on the cross. From: insouciance – light-hearted unconcern.

ARTIST
ACTOR ATHELETE POET PHILOSOPHER SCIENTIST SCHOLAR

Pack. Hurry.
We must go.
We're special attractions
at the go-on Chateau.

WALK IN THE PARK

A youthful jaunt in the county park,
loose, follow freedom bare.
Two couples eager, bowers apart,
Love whistled new-found share.

Brown in gold as a tossed brass knocker,
coat on hills told of bold hot summer.
Round players heads spun heat like lacquer,
that finished in gulps of full slack laughter.

Fair youth, quick, discover in custom
guards slack, at lunch in there tower.
Book of life, open, bear on breeding;
think then, to put off teasing.

 Many the years since first full tingle,
retrieve value, its bout with propriety
in years-since single and call on excitement to battle satiety.

There, Reveal, magnificent usurper, embarrassment ignorer,
master of secrets, trowel shy and spread your base,
oblige society's been-long-after to keep the fit of men

who end toward tries, no great blunder to crop done;
who banish surprise still spot stunned
where No, is so miserable and knows it,
Love, let off its no-love ledge, on account,
finds untroubled prosperity a marked fit.

So, in honours, speech, manner, many lax;
climbs much mentioned Reason, advocate in tallow flax,
that gives love back, the rhinestone bidden.
Sex in this may be outcast, never hidden.
The friction-fires that shape animal life,
If only as mornings' promise to night,
vie never so long till again are risen.

SURPRISE ACROSS A WAY

The couple with the shifting house
were down in the brush gully
picking the arms and feet of the fire-ripe fruit.
Too, Mountains move so houses must.

Behind a glass asleep; one cough, two,
for the pluck of soot-treat yesterday bought
with run along rush road.
    There was only the run you see!

Looking for some assist from popping around
bursts of inspiration that had some failed,
tease and twist of ever-loving after-work yawn,
would fine tune a static sea.

  Then a point of stork
moving to a moving beat
revealed one long-neck fellow, behind,
all Joe, surprised; worry-wart his going.

The suggestion of that miracle, that uncountable flap
 over many miles (Father always said worry is for naught)
 would air-brush other smiles; that their pass,
 to the sea I think, was a stout poem and not lost on me.

At triumph, what was that but the dig deep!
What worker from a little pain, loss of heat,
could party evening's breathing space,
lift sparkle to baying sun
without the gruff huff at panning ze'd done for it?

If trove cost be sequestered fee; exilic workmen

trussed in memory; holey hood and mantle piece of danger
course stiff mandate, ruse and beg enlightenment;
muse is ordering; so make you check of it!

"WATSON AND THE SHARK"

A disheartening day it was, call for alarum to all horn.
Bright but cloud-filled, saw nine crowd their craft
hearts taxed, hands wage efforts' rescue.
And in the full-sail harbour, grip with ship,
light towers siren calm breakwater
   as one tries test among the shark.

Smoothed by resignation, worry, terror, fear
equipped faces for about to lose life.
Brothers Watson all it appeared, of a father's well-made
grounds and hall; out for a catch,
   harpoon, sound, ready, they watch.

  At odds, thrash alerted others hungry to catch.
  But the rope was caught
and young Watson again touched bell ground.
   Wounded, tale to tell, on canvas captured,
   he would: it showed "how a good and moral man
   might survive adversity" to one John Singleton Copley;
   and light work maybe from another Hand's end.

DEMIOERGOS

In molds doing cast well redoubtable stooper for common weal,
demioergos, Herculean solidement établi, dark rump to able
with petite baron on moral mole hill dog the anger,
as Hermes to those of Smintheus give a stupor and strangles!

Quid domini faciant, audent cum talia fures?
'What shall owners do, when thieves are so daring?'
   When poets climb then fall to quiet?
queries Menalcas before he and Damoetas rapid fire pastorals,
launch on perfect worlds, perfect curls, spiral;
this for that, present; Ho! in that eclogue of Virgil.

Intermediate radars wine as artist cup-catch
of decorative acanthus, foxglove, who'll fence call snide,
ivy-anoint not-napped brow; who now poet,
   so the black hulls come about.

Hence, Excellence, her stout solvents trample fear in fresh simples,
and before call mast, count Buy forgotten habit,
brash the part of Love there. Trials sterile, evidement!
   And leaks goad gravity in agreement to its call.

Notes: demioergos: [Gk.], one who works for the common weal. Solidement établi: solidly established. "Quid domini...Virgil, Ecologue. III. Quia: [F.] –nonplussed.

IMAGE OF MAN ?

On these we matter.
"Mark! cocoon homed," the one to the gathered, "proper upright that
night went with, heightened, hid. 'Who still, their little patch to mend,
dream,' notice and relate among whelps de cognoscenti or not!
Where Lucanus of the many clinks man's tin:
Invidia, hate, jealousy; dilate killer, shameless banner in hand,
long under that excess weight have they,
which too much burden going wrong,
not peace brought,' ever, to any!" ≤1!

   Slip-cousin social maze no more 'sullen art's' choose,
the one now sitting; and origimate somebit 'something meatless!'
   to lead off safe a world, if nouns and verbs... I think you address me!
   As "Et le Tout-Puissant le frappe (smote him) aux main d'une femme
   (by the hands of)" was purled last by God over many a blowing how!
   And of this we sink, only man, may.

"After ego well stumbled on like safe-and-sane berries in Grizzly's field,
all sore and blond, He, She, whatever! Out of the way respectful, were, even!
There, Far from I, to They, success bound; wisdom sunned in silencia.
And at scarce beggary's (b)oister, Tower tries and whigless seventh sage led;
To Author trues True. Whole, agapenor. Be like Christian, later to By-ends
In the Fair `Vanity...' of Bunyan, 'If you will with us to wisdom,
You must leave behind sanctuary.'
"So that now, not just agapenor, but rexanor, many good looks, gracias!
and hovery, ἐξαγγέλλειν exangelein ('Jump! sympathy-with-lies! We've enough!')
you may ward babble choice as slab metal smack insides entire, quibb a terror;
praying trips a-grieve boyhood match to keel star plot ploys that fell fall arrogant.

"And in hound, round sketches, what availed instructs macula where many
a barstool or bakedhead share, topfilmed aflame wi`sa puffing blank mouth,
that now eats overall host, met? – that working planet ever over,

66

as sky's turbid flows schat, cash; flush selfish rote, troubled slight (ownership) that,
from truce inside such settled camp, scorns the torrid baccilae, I!
Who'd, too, for novation Black Lives Do Matter! As all the rest
would their thus, there not! Not there. Not!
As some, like Anteaus, boiled that hour for She, Ma Hearth
(glad for the gifts and show) would, goding; we too,
with eyes attune a wood turned agewood exercise,
that slurs it a freshet of brutal badgood warms to boast;
soil and bark goat got, run to overturn; and why immeasure Heart
do you bold good king Standing otherwise drop?
await lack Precedent, emphat, that fires wingless spirit herself,
standing heat of fire flight across acid sky; as we ourselves oil
T. Spall's JMW Turner – salutes accept, do! - Death there, other maker,
'his debt-to-collect, armoured; our painter, hero, shield-less,
laughing last labours "The sun is God!"'s us, and dies?!
Well just that! And who," glimmering, "will - if any of ancestors' thoughts,
said, ever, of light, any of it, got through – not understand that?
 Even as some are yet to shore beyond white. As still others,
with 2's & 3's; and streets all New York or back to the `40's Street Cars,
seen in the late Fifties, early Sixties of that eras' envious in Los Angeles?
Who, which really, when was that? Then, or just yesterday? I Stoke! But hold!
Think of and have it: as bold old excess-carbon finishes into cloud over,
and bastards do!? But for control, are still in draft of hope.

  "And oh! If more spirited, yet less pocket-relevant,
like thin mor not sure; long asaddle [Windows buffered – 'as addle.'
A detection most curious for serendipity & insight
Into mere sound of language, ye old beacon thrice ""overagainsts"
Inflection in lived life."] …I say… asaddle a hard pan,
disbelieving Divines' interventions are made into belief
as bid-fortune storm leaves its firmament and helps drop.
So, worse hires and their guarderies are bettered by the Way of angels,
all ten Orders, fallen and minion 'by the Beatific Vision of Truth himself,
of Truth taught' and will, I say go. Or not.

As love, vast ordinance, deem stretch of self on such dry deck tautly,
as saves a world!   And I do Care! So holler Must.

"That if was clear non-preservants holding crayon'd sheets –
picturing the towns and countries round, individual and similar –
nothing north of selfish, all south vile cloth wave have brought, bring;
armed response at flout, hurt of one kill, one you, Black, of which
there's but this throughout here in amer… where if any of it Fair/Equaled up is,
democratic For The People-general, which is the all, us, They would themselves,
whites, seeing from this, that other end, or just the knowing of what they know
"Of the Ever now, down-push – and scream for from African Americans
to be the most fully armed. But opposite, you against again, I say,
these little! So hate-filled (- my squirm to question, uncovered, teller on)
nothing was would not against in uniform,
in that mono-tint culture of ghastly, greatless hearts,
that you may have once bought as ream; trekked long, hard
and wore as nard armed among in same crank foldery!
I believe we must call who, on that!"

Shrug? Sure! Thinking, that's what I've always meant,
by - all who in Western lands sit, live, gross inhumanities on, in
are in fact as good or bad as white boys. So call that!
As speak outagainst "Such troths, keeps others out by the bay,
Downtown club, campaigne and non-poetic chat realized
of prized timeless peasant hook, yet! Also, donation side (he continued,
as moon un-limned mind going satis liquet.) That there judge-free Elysium,
illicit by the un-listening; " said said-snatchworm hid bottom,
and "These will stand?! groveled grovel-masters close enough
to catch the cough and waft of cruel delay cast golden; not cast golden!
(our interpreter madly interpolating.)
　　But Love, sweet, voiced a No! Un! That could the whole sever amend
　　half-histories they'd adopt; scuts of inaccuracy and air-in-screams where
　　the soldiers and firefighters came back, bought, for camouflage blues'
　　now new against The People! Insistence,

Ill-human heretic. Which, yellow by the bay yellow citizens
   grew the make of No government!
Becoming more confused; do I trip, fall in the disjoint,
of all this I thought: a way to save man? But why? I'm nobody.

Then the slight one standing, in the mess of sense and interpretation;
and not slight our comparison, having watched, more coarse cast:
   "Lights! – Than studies and home?   Widths of brought, kept left!
   Mighty par, amenable tasks that soothe livery, board, very blush
   of better tea in cups, every immigrant, every land: Ho! not?
   And that, toward good for a time crowd on!? Yes that!
   For Time, Ready Time does tractless track! As know.
   And such questions examboard, able stand! un-Yank untone desperate\
   scrawling winners lost. He, framed. You Wall enter soft,
   scramble outer-technica, which, bears it pedestrian,
   Even berserker idris, even here, sees grab cup, watch watch, decide.
   Fame, the snare, hidden hands with have, Stabilize!
   and hoe your draughts dear!"

Continuing, brow-raise in interlude, "Aileroning life's toil in that then
   caught out, let, lay Lend and Have beware imploits that slight
   O skipping seconds! where might injustice go willing with
   out of doors for willing rapes, and avoid! As the Small live there.
   The less than could would. Who, any mead of drowsy corridors
   for love of just-their one, sectioned truth, ladders-up struggles of
   we, whole, us of, not! - That mid and opposite-Midas creed of greed,
   the less-character the makeup of His, isn't!

"And Refresh!" more, "For, are lasting, and say Touch us! if not swept,
   and see are Lifeous! Not another unpatriot simulac special interest,
   fallen cities born hard on. Minorities by majorities shown dog-chased wild;
   the near-pitiable army one weapon makes.   And Initial purpose:
   to protect the vulnerable; recollect Eleanor's commission back;
   where are robbers in the land, giants to themselves bland;   69

their followers throughout, Worldwide, the big-handed prefer;
and the sick selfish pity that's – in allowance against-the-song-of-Everything,
who and she Redoes that newly adolesce on posterity's broad smile,
always-cynic, chugs a Hi! Again Precedent, having seen for itself
too-short a while, and in sigh deflates close on a ground, just so,
inhales under breathe measure close skies
and pushing widths beyond restful molds' blind drive
accepts rendering Dance with song further for a while.

"And it's still un-be-luckin'-leaveable for you can! Descend near.
Oh! near enough! And tell rots' rob-giant," this one continued,
"in surly misdirects, sniggles into sleeve do not unnoticed
in your stream these days go.
  That self-trust, under not-so-boundless immature, sent scorched,
ever-duplicitous, always backward, conservative rush and shoot
of a crooked piled-on smile ("It's about heritage!" he'll...) "Yeah!
And stolen, so free, for you, stuff!" the people membrane: "we know it!")
whizzed, banged, to get his best out of is supplied many material.
But Erictho allowance to squat more, her desolate rock there,
Rescinded! Done! These Cato lux !'"
"That, in it, beware your back!" The first firmly, "for these callow
enantions, like the dalliant Hollyfield/Romney oiothen,
(remember?) enantibion, in anti of life, fake or not,
Ever fialisco will stand in here! Of the retinals! What!? To query But,
remember! In life and serious trues, equal in match like a man,
  alone with feet and hands Johnny stand? Where's the evidence?
He will not! the batters Good and Pure of Good inhabits,
any field of play or war! Where you say you have seen males kill,
shame, hurt women, children;
  add who are old and in some way less-than-fair-to-be-putupon,
persons, places or things, far away or up close, maybe unless fired-on!
And that there in that, you have seen a man? And I, you. Never! No! NoT!
In no timeplace! Save among slither, bottom-feed, boredom buff,
equid-forced self-haters; whose dangerous buffoonery

70

into the exposed flanks of civilized men's lives goes boring on.

"Yet, still, none want to be hurt and only a fool enters a fight not expecting same.
And nope. Many won't stand lest in a crowd, though the look would tear!"
 Dark worry closed on squinting brow they were beginning to make sense -
"They'll shoot in the back. Pick the weaker; not-men killing boys as said,
aa male or female calls, reports on or posts from whites or others conspiring
on stone-turned networks, etc., to the living as that, bring of police cops,
all society's envies and distrust, dis-ease rally really, still against,
the most worthy of the worthy called, by, through, because of
emergency debt to Firsters owed. And solidement!
 That blank internet, in false-pulse-false interior, terror presents! But more!
Will, if you do not stop them, set escape-proof kills;
excess monies behind wicked blinds AI black face robot purchase;
and post, as allege of mastership, the soft courage in picture –
the un-alias'd scarddy cat!"

Seeing unease ease and brow bright, he, Whose now sic, pile, I continue,
Reports from every broadcast falsely on. Try to commercialize; grab advantage
and side-eyes', as said. Knowing you pay for it. Who drills whole gift and very life
out `a the rest.   Which is Mine
`till beasts and beautiful waters short homes abort;
and griots: algae, tree, brush, grass, who, we - very Life carpet, and Air,
it seems the wretch never grew up on; where the poor man = dignity's loss,
scatters through a thousand tunnel vortices that never-truths caught,
sent or came. And, of this? Be wryly full citizen
as Time, positive teacher, even stiff-necks purse
and to/against true-beasts' be brought. Being the treacherous
at-with most-apparent to not-able, that in turns of ins to outs,
unjust-assess air of solidarity, with in-line hate – in "country back"
and "there was a time…" scared, oh were scared! So killing thus!
with red Windsor, bald blue baldric, to wire distemper to ooze\
a signal! thought, from the royals (Though late there's a Harry acting Human.
and a Charles may be yeoman.) for all hoped better from royals   71

a-fuss death's tolerances, poor themselves, those many imbalanced year.
As the gold-having instructed all but selves.

And these, as these are the same who not a crockborn Christmas,
wresting in sidle, from all the little mothers all their smaller pennies
missed, everywhere! World-wide. We expect to market ourselves
to your industry in turning this, but must ask, I'm sorry?
Can we depend on you? Accept with faith; bet the farm; attain a Yes!
To the bank or as gospel take this your ascent? Have you given it?
Will those eggs... that dog... I can't say the word: squawking!
 Do I lose it? Is, agreement? Or a bad caught hunch? - "Yes! Yesss!"
I, beginning again to lose the stretch, then snaps I out of it!
But then by sorts, at rush to words in, in a struggling
to stay awake, point, by such bambi road
to Last Lighter's lamp in her eye, in which
we have seen the evening primrose, and she is't beauteous!"
Yes, there are distracts, I. But will You accustom to whole-Good
and loud-Truths, the needy bill, who profane through the land,
themselves tilt?" Yes! Yes! As evening passed;
others, to their wives, waxes, wanes, wombles, I stayed,
sitting mid field, with the thought: oscillating truth or farce or both?
What was accomplished here?
As the slashing purples and yellows of ceilinged finally-coachless skies set.
Through which I thought I saw Divine, to his Bench, for rests.
Odium and chance? ...more feelthought than... But turned away at that.

Notes: Invidia; Lucan's De Bello Civili Bk. I; L.69. "Et le Tout Puissant..." Judith on
Hollofernes. The Tower, W.B. Yeats. '...If you will go with us...' John Bunyan's V. F. ἀγαπήνορ:
Lover, host, welcomer of men. ἐξαγγέλλειν (exangellaen) to bring forth word (αγγέλ – Greek
root of angel, messenger. Anteaus: Giant of myth. Mor: humus layer. `By the beatific...'
William Langland - the long, lean, crazy fellow...; P. Ploughman - Notes (p. 165) Penguin.
Satis liquet: it sufficiently appears. Erictho: arch-witch of Thessaly consulted by Lucan's
Sextus Pompeius, ibid. Oiothen: (foot to foot), face to face. Wombles, wambles, nausea.

WORLD TRADE

From Congo, the latest most whipped, to Nubia to Egypt,
who with their bodies spell out you're order.

If New York checked herald drowsy world,
and eyes that stared in were aghast selfish sin
how did reaction in that change and borrowed suit of time
not hold better Will sent by all at the crime?

If they had cause the incident and released their fear in draughts,
left hearts at ports' edge, how did others, in charge and against,
their direct opposites, not seal the entry and foil the tear?

Then what good the teacher hours allot on a price,
appearance and scent of spoil?
Turns were from policies worn to those foregone;
and no relief for anyone shaking fist, chasing charms
against humanity's faithless wrongs.

You may forward wake nights, calumn sounds
and dive sights gnash in head; pause on the answered why,
trail little entry, little material, little by the grace
which was what you ungraciously ate.

Note: Calumn: from calumny – scandal, etc.

À LA CHINE

From the train all flushing between tracks
are not of the refuse, disease nexus.
        But I would grow tigers out back;
        pack gangly containers with pristine habitat and send them

with clean air in a thousand trillion backpacks or baby strollers,
or biting toys back.   If history barks the path,
if scarcely escape that, then you can be affirmed but the spotty trust

in another continent's forests, along a simple river's hijacks,
and the seneschal courts that once wore it. If a less-humane
and caring camp, like bad weather has you trapped, we wish
sturdy hats, and your and our humanists back.

Note: seneschal: servant or agent in charge of feudal lands for a lord, etc.

THE PULL BACK

Bark off.
Girder showing.
Limb.

SLEEPY WILLOW TOUR

In our state of affair, windy side of a take,
if in business suit or not, it was said, angels wait,
be careful with yourself. You are not a god!
Keep your water back and flat against
tin eye catches higher rates of filch on poor,
fletches them loose darts in catchless skies,
to stick where neither care nor grace exists:
that bitter bark: switch, bate, catch.

Timeout! Breakable bowl of charity, in stitch,
has, in red cart rid with sore hearts
to make women and men of they
whose shineless plod on human time
seems lygun Pylian, full radiance agoreten line.

Handlers, from bow to put-on, snuff candle the otherwise out;
that one of the first wisdoms, of doing to the world,
as you would have done to you, away stiffpliable
stifles done light, or the one from Heraclite – "wisdom:
speak the truth, act naturally." shall not
by but two sides be brought when clearly the thing is a box.

And there fine masters, singing carol, going round,
suggests of boot-strap with, as some our fond,
nutritious scrap eat, enjoy the paid entertainment,
wash, splash and wash away of good helps,
true cureless-pocked medicines,
swaddled corporate bargains of broken contracts,

sworn to the warm blood, sweet sweat Love creates;
settle with Excess and False Argument
on attention Divine hates - of at all costs win!   75

It a sphere flake makes; reports of success rarely ring.
   Sleepy Willow flex!

Men forget how much at Wind's buffets you track.
Fact is, with you as, saying again: whose past intelligences
current ones do not prevent; looking, we feel ourselves
gods again.

Notes: "Nestor, Ligun Pylian Agoreten – Nestor, clear-voiced Pylian.(from/of Pylos) orator –
Homer, Iliad.

BURDEN

There is a being so; there the good don't lie.
      Yet it was who vaulted oil, high, to disperse,
fill waste tube, smoke noxious stack?
      They were digging that!

Did tipple together, the 'sloven tikitack,'
      that un-armoured personality could churl,
glam hug and drivel in build-love's stable,
      a feel for other in self lost to fine-horse stutter-able?

When at prowess
      lending gent to done-down,
came shy imponderable with stout it might tithe
      as possible was denied and from tried.

Ground drums the demon swivel,
      back-to-equilibrium charges disable,
so antennae, wing, horn, fin, leaf, heart survive.
      They had become that?

At hour certain,

       buckskin hills' line cursive,

the natural state unlocks dark hearts

       and no more Black males are blackma(i)led?

By whoever love to say it, long lost giggle,

       in selfish or look-at-me chide.

Their animal persons for themselves blind tied

       who piercing third eye in lieu of reveals

find lion and tiger and Stamphilian Jay

       where fear of no man stands

dealing sharps for flats. And that must suit

       our Menelaus, and he will have to hold

`til sighs with their lady come back home!

       Poised to upset, straight at table

cater down what hates the difference in men.

       And the best way into calm is still from a storm.

THE GREAT CONVERSATION

Enlarge, you are not unedged, embryo to authority in wears,
or stricken damnatio from hearts to be found,
or that Before you these things hadn't been, said.
Add are the one mind in serial with else. ≥1.

From lethe-wash babe and bundled to same shore,
prized, penned on a strand, new champions to restore and make came.
Ten of these after nine of those; and wears head you'll crown
called contemplation. So that Maecenas lift! Megathumon!

Your great discuss endures,
has a steady visage, right grace.
Un-available to silence here, fear wants position,
and casts with sharp epithet pretension, in need.

'Utterance being enough,' exposition will take pinnacle
with the "old of renown"; craning to influence influencers.
And after the flood Divine even worried
'they will be "restrained by nothing...."' so scattering came and went
for men from that place, weightless in preponderance
of souls that builded with the stone a mud.

And if shame was to be handed out all that time
why did so many cross ire-meridian
of accusation and solitaire from counterpart?
Great Conversation you've propped!
And Meaning, you've bridged cataract to nourish starvelings!
Je résiste pas!

Notes: "Utterance..." – From an 1834 R.W. Emerson letter to T. Carlyle. Megathumon:
great heart, soul, mind, etc. I resist not!

In The S^*t

With back against the wall to assist, you can do aught
but this: spell blame and shame to falling down Joe!
You can see now lie rolling hills that to jagged peaks lead.
Even here, attained idyllic, all are under strained attack
from the monsters Want made – relationship, belief, diet, work,
thought and tool! The [place? Full of fool]!
   Some things make you bark!

Well, few are paying survivals' basics any attention.
So, say what you should, cut the shuck!   Tell 'tis current!
To studio, hall, theatre, and chamber filled with learned guests –
Learned in what their governments lent; unstudious scratch,
scrabble, scamble and shim shoddy shear enshankment!

Truly courier, was half your meaning in the war rooms! In,
get me some scramble author who in tangle and toy said a lot, that you said!
Let the self-conscious riot and outstream the most meaning. Heart to heart,
Mind unqualified, such like! And may incind braziers not with coal or wood
crackle with the smoke they'd spun.   There, not undone, will you why as wind?

- This is where that dinner you told, one with the bear, where went past intent!
Poor ripped Grizz, to match fly, as you sat out of but got planted in memory, yes? -

Yes! Much in memory! And I tell, There is a price on everything.
Conceive it – person, place, or thing, and it, at least to mind,
in some form appears, even in the no-form of prior, with its opposite.
Here and now or where and when.   So, we consume like the sot,
which is formant. And wonder our enrollment. You wanted to speak to them,
say what learned from trying. But they had s*^t in the air, and water! where?
Hell, you don't know what-the-pluck! But pretty, it weren't!

Augh! Maybe the couch Is better than hard ground for sleep's purpose   79 to some! To others, not! You be of the not! And buff as bum!

Wild Wow! with your hum. Landleaping, awayfarring,

walk your two thousand William with the angry gait!

Seek retribute in the hurt Samuel, cleave the tie and sad shirt!

What the f*^k with the angry blurt pickitivant? 'Tis a crowded place next?

Blowing to air of parts and well?? Red waters vent? Or from behind, more;

via the gathered mean ingenite, with torch and fork, which the same thing Is!?

Et Je savais que ce jour viendrait!   And I knew this day would come!

The usual card-hand trick was!   Where's the truck?

Watch the hand – you look – Not this! And in shaking off the first,

to grab rung the meaning, lose both on the washed revel shore,

miss the if, lose it. Fall.   And the trick and wicked trial team on.

Notes: Word excavations from Robert Burton's Anatomy Of Melancholy, New York Review
Books, New York, 2001 (Glossary): - scamble: to struggle, to get along somehow. Incind: to
kindle, inflame. Pickitivant: a pointed beard. Ingenite: inborn.

UNHAPPY

Demetrious Marc Duvernay-Moore

It was the inconspicuous day through which, at interval, disaster came
facing with grim vehement, un-sheathed weapons, yelling love for absence.
It took no time. And 'came mid-sentence' like all significance,
in plain dissemblance and brown torn wrapper. `Till yellow from bottom
with pain squint outcame unbelief believed.

Somnolence those days, stared the light, on the corner, the longest,
caught in swirl's "it can't be'!" Discovering tail's known circumference,
Claudel had been in for professorships' and shellings.
We felt heart-holed but resigned!
'Omar was there - his Iliad still; firebrand Whistler, new with rub shocks.

And lest option least with again lived, ruining, alternately singeing
and curling gimp share, we enjoined the gone as we've always done,
to move quickly on and do what work there needs done.
        Meaning at sire gate at some run,
and you have left the man, where he came in Son.

WITNESS

Something dark about this light, you very buck and willing kick,
do exact-for-the-riches trample.
I like us in the wild country. Wrecked qwerty
and slide fury to destruct under us.

This slide, adorable from a rivered parking lot,
Lost no time scaring.   But now, how? Don't know!
We defended, and gallery cut from the pages all right,
that bias lift pressed to turn Witness for the prosecution.

So cleared court's never smoked in time nor accident,
smoking, laid mind to verdict.

Was guilty, clear. But guilt from heap, burnished, placed nice
under Not For Sale sign kept,
when the populous that citizenry coulda cried but didn't,
and viscous verity, black cloak a mash of dust,
back to everyday forgetful cussed.

We were assured of your confidence in this. Will you
honour that?
I might, said the bad man, if you stop offering me light!

  Shortly after writing this I thought, I've analyzed myself! But maybe not!

S TUDY

May be a bit of a slog, but I'd like to counsel
another read once afoot and three quarters through -
when - wouldn't usually de-closet beforehand, 'cept
what uncovered thus far is manifest significant –

Jean-Jacques's "Emile." What a study on education, mindful!
And more than suggestion for youth.
Any, at any stage in human evelopment being honest
could precise commodity - notwithstanding scientific,
'near-moral,' existential and other misses – find
in these eighteenth-century book;
as step-drawn pictorially as Plato's "Republic" on its subject.

Curiously here and there strong disagreement caught found
with this other 'plain man' only to de-cave a little further on,
to find fuller explanation and no disagreement;
where the hand that turned out hidden light now had it going on;
and recommend his tome do I full on. ≥1.

CALLIRHOE!

    The all in for men, Aman among, me says
I can talk to you `cause you're not the wife, girl-friend.
    Eer(ily) felon traitors seek the people's approval.
And your beautiful name is in verse as assistant paid, this holy
of so many holy days; as I suit you Erectheum your close-held temple.
    - But Callirhoe, is it surely you? Of the beauty, goodly flows, passages,
doings, movements; Oceanid and daughter of two rivers
who was by the Momus, whoever s/he is, of Literature mentioned
(so much for notes prodigious on books' pages and nifty back lots)?
  Were you ever not, with celebrity, in the ancient world of nature?

Some earliest sights were Hesiod's, which Aesop and Early human knowledge
Africa from, with early humans at gallop point, speak to, of –
And keep and hold that best King AND Queen of continents'! Black Man!
Your Charge! (Lord God! Nile, whole continent try drain? Do I asiding.
Amazon? Mississipp..? Indus? Yangtze? Yawlue, Yellow – God...s to us!
(Thus, do Tree greet thee! As She pleases Ma Aerth!) as also generally from
Lower India and Earth's, darker, earliest, southern base persons; seafarers,
that All from private perspectives, paid north to Egypt, central Asia, The Americas.
  Isles north the Pole South immediate, that other time attested to?

A-wail, someone cried, Mother, daughter, maiden, oh the wasted time-given?
'Maybe!" She, 'But Defenders of Good, call them of the holy Croesus sort,
men need! Whom themselves surfeit, sacrifice, even betrayed in love;
themselves out, than stand with vengeance at blind love's anything- at-once
/wants\, betrayal; for the good continuance of the race,
  A Christ! of the highest regard, good unselfish behavior.

- Callirhoe polished---- Now for your son Ganymede!
Aquarian, satellite Jupterean; bearer-to and beloved by Dios –
in good Xenophon's Socrates - for the mind, soul – psyche – way.
Even as Virgil with others in assault sat out with his "...et rapti Ganymedis...'

'...and ravished...' - a pretty fast blame we peek!

So, my bright Demetrious, Sun too me, son mine now!
Who, to my once repeat of the Know Thyself cure,
"You always say that!" "What do you mean; what are you saying?"
To which of-less-convince, I: How the old request, was but balance,
for the living. Of life for ones', as well as others, all's sake.
   So, Ayn badly interpreted! From said wake-start, finish, -
which is what is said now - Callirhoe, Lycian Lady fond of Diomedes,
the only soul-dier at Troy, in going-beyond to be by Apollo admonished
for his striking at gods, as he'd done Aphrodite, 'think again...
seeming allowance despite, such a thing in no part would be let...'

Still, Doings beautiful! Take part! Victory is with if will try be that!
 - Surreptitious? Quick tempers pack! Actual murderous? On the iron bus!
And quicker, those most with humanity's commons: let selfish, immoral lacks,
perspirate mid loud boos out back. Not a grace among `em.

CHRONICLE: GROUND-JUMBLE ANNALS – APPLE SIGHS
(Mind Wars, Middle Years) - 27 March
Year of The Pledge; 11:26 GMT.

Upper helm, full sprite, combed stretched the clouds
as made of pissoir a back lot, and on fair ground burst component parts.
No more wholes. Icarus, a while! Trysty balustrade palmed going up,
at run against that day.

Inside, task and subtle mask straight, Chirper, conversy in upper porch,
in squidgit, squidgit, squidgit, to squidgit, squidgit, squidgit
gets squidgit, squidgit back, this hour, so stops; cold draft mind to mind
through the roof, took half a minute. 'This idiot is talking back to me!?'
But of the squidgitsqudgitkluck, squitcheerugh,kukukugrilgrilshrishirughs
squidgee, nothing from me; like baffle 'flips' by an a & many t.

Pig brigand near the bridge snorts. Collecting pledges, re-evaluate: No!
On mound beyond! As fourd, daudge, and specially chevrolate's exclusions
'This is our country!' spoil-brat'd the 9-11 dis-rally rap-up; with No,
not a single Darker portrayed, days, when trip 'all mumsy' hit the fan
and message received sent, so hurt squeal, 'and the moan gave out raves.'
`Cause all the Black men and women, in business suits helping shocked cops
and every-color colleague out attritious towers made heart! those days,
as 'civilization', unseeing, resumed buckle atrocious, that met
unrestricted camera's gaze; soon disfavored; to cradle division, markets,
distrust; what else visible truths excluded, set-against; to un-abstruse
and keep battering blanco worlds. Dusty givers, mere human?
Not again in tender gifts pictured, so the Critical, now clearing libraries,
could fit same purpose.
    Larger-draw go nowhere in run! Word golden slaps cranial hum!
- A nascar horn along gully's gunnels gaffing goes off;
ultra-busy chicks cluck; splurge Nature Indestruct, catches self
    leak catch for Her dress, fluff for a nest, control aside set,
on tough nearby rough to grow from; whose factory there,

in honeycomb, has a leaf in dehisce five years on, commanding curls;
and more seem a Barbary treasure wound in a wind on trail beyond.

So, it's where assisted helpless where could, should, would we record
≥ 1 soldier for republic proud, coxcombed or not,
realized farmer frenzied fresh of 'designing' government
now tapping the taped roof, for assists, wherein
were equal to tasks, where Life put momently in!

Gone crippling pledge, merchant edge unpreserving,
and one-tailed tests and cares, slight, oh major! There you were
believing as Thoreau in Emerson's woods,
neither too fortunate nor palatial;
of slat, mortar, brick, soul and body lain against a fine shiver;
where life put momently in. Apple sighs and the good bid normalized!
\Ěnd observation

Note: Crippling pledge: Michea 2; 10 – loan that works hardship on the borrower.

SOMETHING TO COMPARE

All profits disappear: ...
We hunt the cause of ruin, add,
Subtract, and put ourselves in pawn;
For all our scratching on the pad,
We cannot trace the error down.

What we are seeking is a fare
One way, a chance to be secure:
The lack that keeps us what we are,
The penny that usurps the poor.
Theodore Roethke; p/o "The Reckoning"

And about the old rag disused in analogy;
neck hairs stood magnetic raise as at a distance
against scours and rubs; wings of scam through'd ghetto fair.

In ragdom money clothed, shawls washed hands, did pat backs.
Meals served at haunts-discards crows clasped as freedom
in the close mesh of collection company years,
    from lay-in-wait, coarse their elevator gears

like shareholder sycophants that socialize into bank,
insurance co gone, in guarded all-done, all-their kingdom.

Meanwhile, twilight golds' and brightsomes' air
winning breezes bought. At home in poor districts
tan hides stay torn apart.

Self-interest capitalism needs reduce, cheap labour,
more for them, and something to compare,
more purge treasure from-The-Poor's-heart-and-flank sought.
They have a bad-to-worse-actors-that-everything-Good-upset caught.   88

That cold sold separate through the present shows The Poor,
all fixed out on prayer; their players, so buoyant they float
for new plays on a field.
   Challenge them ronin! Roughshod among run.
   Lest show none were there, as the show goes on!

CLEAR AIR

Man persists in bunting his troubles and their solutions Father;
it is no applausable sacrifice for The Whole.
  The selfish do not act out of care.
   Must the poet always pull a tear?

And yet, in this there is an avalanche effect.
One can limit one's abuse-of-environment use,
but, "I have to get across town!" Or "This field needs plow,
and most-offensive of exhaust is my only how!"

Well, men are in places attempting to change that.
Because they can see cause and effect; and the other animals
are angry and or laughing at, and are not complete tools.

  Though somewhat quiescent tardy end, I (your son)
having attempt of measure of self with written word
and extracting joys of contemplation in approved aloneness,
finding there the manly thought, sentiment of poets, thinkers,
philosophers surfing time – the life of mind determined.

No race, as you know, but consistent helpful Marathon.
 - While where readers are, are wished
    unobstructed views of the near.
 - Here, sun-sparkle in undisturbed snow, blanket that cures

89

to sink and to high air run blessed atmospheres create
quiet simple and play part the un-offender pleasure infused.
This one has spoken of clean air importance, to a pester,
his tongue sore's in the affair.
   But we motile on, because lives live there.

CROW VISITS

   At the 'stone threshold of the winds' stood she,
one Darnella Frazier watching the conversations of the clouds.
 He sang (even before Hughes) Crow knows everything.
Got it all mapped! The curious un-guarded secrets,
and suggests Ted's photo-mimic of Crow's
Crow's-foot peer an exact careless representation.

Fear? Crow knows it not. Safety first will him out
of exchange of attack when groaning fly offs
happy or angered yet upright
child and confessor his reflector Black.

At the county dump gaining refresh from a house without,
passing the trash-compact operator, Crow in his own chair hopped,
   even as within arms' reach passed.
 Here the poet's laugh and shake of head at self in that.

So, of that operator had to ask, 'Friend of yours?' 'Pet?'
 Only half-shake negative and shrug, with impression left,
Crow was visiting and relaxed from Crow's own confidence.
Here is self-thought Wittgenstein's 'Don't think. But Look.'

Crow said, I have one neighbor's chicken-coup on watch.
And patrols I another's doves out, using as close-near

your bee-bee gun yard, activator! I said, With eyes and ears,
I see and hear that! Victory and protection!

Butterfly, god of feints, skipped by. Crow this time shrugged,
old cold eye kept. All things sit their platform, he, Ground of being!
Hope for that spark that animation is. Is electric magnet chemicals spryly
savor that often flavors fields of rays frequent. Still more, ultra-violet to decay
to nothing much. Save all the rest opposite not it. You or I. You
not you Markov Blanket. They the eye-spies in I fulfilment.

There will be a day, he kept going, You will be out or not
and the neighbor's doves will be in the pine. It being neighbor's doves pine time!
Someone on the left, smaller, a whistle chant lays, alarum, and almost
a huge sheet of paper crumpled at once, or like from inside a truck bustling
merch on, or thunder break ... anyway, right, wild flight,
all forty forced pinion leave tight. Sharp slice beige-white
a tunnel only he could, wizard while, out-early Owl
precise a tree at chase will incise. Now turning, see
just in case, returns he to fall-through break-upon position.
 But nope! All Gone! So Back to bandy Barn.

Also, your hands may be too wash of dirt, a thirst that sharely drew you!
 Where we were, There was earth. Sky blued dark, it was all pretty and health!
But Georgia is Georgian And Is?issipi? Disconscious? Minne what? Flori who?
 Forgive me Native You!

I shook my head and said, It's brilliance how the big bees sometimes come
stealth without buzz, and the open spaces hum.
I said, I think of how Tetrarch made me cry all day, when first I heard `em!
Growl, Thrash, Bang! Grunt, not a single un Heavy moment or bit of stunt!
My marvel account. And "I did not want that to end!" Mat, has been me
Every time! Anthem, non-burlesque Epic, Rage, Address the Public that art is!
Speed Grunt Growl! Pith and Pitch! I love Metal!   Did I say I need the growl,
lyric and Disturbed Indestructible, speedy guitar hands riff and warrior stance?   91

Add Rage tear of Joy, and 'We don't give a shit!'?   Crow laughed.
I straightaway went back. I had gone far. And this was a man Crow treated such,
playing amusements to heart's stop.

Crow said Caw! I've had by enough but as go, tell, Is not direction dimension
through the cash floor of life? Are not your seed-wished solecisms like ice cream
on the stifle field of seems? And man! is he not the melt 'burlesque'
one philosopher* said is? Did twangs the net, drag-knuckle hate spewers reach?

 All questions proved rhetoric with his one-hop fly off.
 At the hold circling with others seeing spiccato - as I ear bent,
he sniffed chortled Nothing but trash for us is of worth there among them!

 Another day. In the sun, for any cloud, Crow thinks Hawk is a chump!
Dip Dive Crow sets up angles comin'-at, pecks harass of Hawk until something
got! with Crow's last attack. So off, Out! he. As Hawk completes her circles.

 Note: *A. Schopenhauer. Spiccato – [L.] Spicatus, spicare, arranged in spikes etc.

COFFEE

His third, or comes slumber intact.
Under sharp congest, work to do,
costs him humdrum caution.
But keep craves them basement-
to-floor ceiling creates he did scold;
and lost to steals from the people,
no more green-face captures hungry bail,
but full-care crate, carts equal
suggests he to himself those hungry days.

For so the yell drama relates bleak dharma
beaks and whistles against wall there. Eliminator,
grandiose accounts sequel, and scans the why you were there,
relieved, chairs and stools well sat good, green mornings, Who ya!

Note: Dharma: Hinduism-duty by observance/custom; divine law, etc.

THREE

LOVE AND GOOD WRITES

Hyper dream, no fear carpet,
like that sent one king of men woke from rest.
We drop inhales, some weightless fare cohese:
a broken bias?

Fair gentlewoman, all meanness a-heap,
we wanted to see and hear you.
While offending-clay curled curtaining faces;
a delight not upperhouse without dislike,

eked of we heavy eye lids, fanning
these black, your white which
in a similar Johnson night Jack fought `em,
Joe discomfited; disgusted heads donned swivel.

But you, kind soul afar, do the let being good writes.
Dust should drape from infinite objects here.
They've leave! And covenant loose you now
in this uncivilized place!

THE ORIGINALS

Early in the year, late in winter, that snows
like one's up and down, soft intelligencer,
should for man's possibilities be falling, seems right.

Recover twice Positive! Not because are the only thing
of shine in mean un-bright, but because believe
it solid in existence and the rightest right.

Inexorable flow of life's directions wills to good creation and
Good Mother Dark, less-bright just now, loving, not-void expect,
like ripe summer's gifts, fresh nourishment from the garden are.

   That had to get out counsel of years. And don't know of Words
or translations or what was actually in hearts that copy mind
the prop of ages, and out-live inhumane stasis,

like any that have, of themselves given gift of contemplation,
a Pythagoras, a Camus, a Wordsworth instance, finding such knowledge
that is the remembering of the remembering self.

Quiller-Couch, so timely, of the many who suggested
one read not only critiques and academic condiment
of the vast work of right thinkers, they whom we pray love Creation,

but the Thinkers themselves. The source. That you should
be at least that honest with the world. Yes, you've gushed excited
discoveries and can barely get into own centuries.

Virtues of assistance, spoken of again and again, will stand angry glare
as post as outcast; that even the knout and being the being broken
upon the wheel of 'keep quiet about that!' when honest, that struggling people
will find through un-health's mad onslaught will not dally out.

For so long doubt watered impolitic fear-of-error and kept man
grapple dishonest caresses of dollar, that he has nearly always
missed himself at entrance to his better beginnings and healthier count.

But how will scatterings of thought be received among the people courted
by careening whim and money thrown at?
 That seems not the always question, and I know I have circled and lined
and high-lighted this times before; but it is the giving of right thoughts thinker
that weight and heft have, not complaints simple in the massive affairs of men.

And right thoughts, the same as that Genevan's designation of a 'good book'
being that text (those thoughts) that exhort(s) readers to goodness,
not re-worked statements made false by whose interests it seems to be to lie,
even 'nobly, to the people that up-counsel.

The descriptions of the heart are at glasses rim and over-pouring
so that less the grammatic and clear progressions are needed by those
after the accuracies of common composition and thought-for-thought;
those that resemble that hearts' turnings and stumbles and pickings up
and embarrassed dustings off, more worthy of our readership and heartfelt,
as many have said.

The corralled, beaten, 'broken' animal of our once helpful-to-mankind,
everything-is-new-and-possible dreams, is now that poor,
downhead creature no rise will be gotten from,
if we've allowed it to be so treated.

Come from the heart mannequin! Leave the brain its careless engines.
It is nearly all chimera, loose talk, and self-preservation over
High, Noble activist Altruism, who is our better, older actioner,
and can only scuff and scuttle the advance of man, who's both previous
and present madness *and* sane possibility we pray to make window of.

FEATHER AND LINE (Save civilization!)

Again! You, cloud? Movement, nutrition, rest;
movement, nutrition; stooping, portendest.
Assaults on a side; american impudence, not done with;
of Life of memoir. 'Matter-wave nature of quantum objects
in there with Taoist 'formal inequality of the standard deviation
of position, to that of momentum. (Change over time of y and x, z...)
(What are you looking at or for?)) Delacroix's natural representation
or wave analysis, has in spin! Keats' Two Things in Mind Held! at 'Once,'
and a cargo prod of gentle, heavenly insight from many a literary power!

Eisenberg's successful uncertainty injects, and the ghost-dance parts
of his calculations command and ask that now, we all to Gödel bow.
With Einstein and Hilbert all! that want me to throw myself out,
Be un Van Halen... well! Wait a while for that~!
that these years guide princely science about?
Why can't that scale? Measure?
'cause it does in each hekastos uptake, tough!

Then in mind, ginger step, deep ruts notch in Newton's carpet,
unavoid! See engine stall or thrust, ray-out, cast or quit...
Say Alternate arena is more on/off, 0/1, pass no pass resistor/capacitor
admonishment to bride man, ensnare earth. Failing... around,
to see better?! Is this, the way of he 'out of true,' stupid who
   a garden for a seat in tinker and inquiry, unmannered?

   Reason abide! Kneel! Descend on kind earth!
of whom only wrenches in the works eye, jamb;
stiff-necks a one! And tell them you Will not, shoe-shod,
adopt non-feel of feet on Deity's haven, cleft, green, pert,
in garnered-agree to civil democratic,
outside the ways of the world's, if need, savvy even?

Go out also and clear for-health hunches across shoulders;
breaks: a tithe-tendency that will dose ya!
Presume, Little One Made, to pay attention now straight up,
on tilt-soon-slide. And action-pay the animal in!
For betrothed; benefact, cloth and water, broth, shelter
of all sister, brother is! Breathe, anxious pushing,
caringly lower stomachs out; intent in good air, none angry!
 But all with Love, in the melee kicking butt in there!

PROPERTY

Broad Earth notice two insistences thread
about a "Y" shaped anchorage
as profits day without.

Shame drives superior from some now
to hunker, builds cower, stand out
der dichter to selfish, quiet shout.

If six be the number following seven
or eight or nine, past eleven,
tame feral beasts you've ridden.

Lay it so by each are seen.
Ground chart you solid crouch on,
so worth, purchased lasso,

steps in strips the does have left;
and catches predator in his dirty business loud.
Awhile, inclined in necessity, forward Forther of Cheer!

SURFEIT
(A Somesense In Who For)

Reason with history would scout the thing
there in every moment ever recorded by organelle,
air, soil, plant, animal, sea or land; some changed since begin,
encompassed and tolled entire range of life and live.

Dual borderless enclosure of the "I" of mind, there, not-there,
Who Is measuring; Beauty rounded more than consternation.
Lacking no fuel, despite late bloom, deadpan choler,
scurrilous flat shoe, and incendiary way
they had in possession, every manner – subtle trepan and idolatry
for word and world could a monster or saint shape;
dry desert scapes, watery tomes – sure, pure,
any frackish friars wandering coupling people among.

Expenses quarreled cadence. Outflow, pigeon to quail
was quick allow to hot seat; who, which and what chief of ancestry often,
when in dream, gave timed kicks – Endurance! for.

But habit heated loyalties - like queen bee, detractors abandoning;
or leader, any land, his people, their willingness taxes
and brash beats the day like the living lights - as that mode
like to troop from battle, exhausted, destitute for sensible liberties,
to passion unannounced buzzed-in yields - caused the wrong,
dry gulp of sun, foul to last drop, where solid and leading citizens
songs to sung, as gladly would. Yet wondered,
would ever amore to pretty homes be welcome?!
Sorrowfully, shared-shard life - diary loose upon teared ground;
fealty-full of never or over-delivered indulgences, accurate analysis,
which rarely so much sign or golden syllable ruled, had fun,
between chocolate treat, fish in heat (cored hope, lucid) -
the bereaved bell near anxious neighbors rarely rung.

Acceptance smiled elf selves; cat tin-roofed;
as vultures meaty treat in wait slept eyeing some.
Attendance off'd toward Annoyance. At gates, bleat heap;
frets fired tools' expectations. But effort moved to correct kiss of death,
muddlemingled, mindmelding with Clarity cheap its seat,
so grew in conscious popular tunes began to hum, even as
pub midden hoplite chambers destructions new in repeats
laid assures; and absence nary a tweet about hoary turn would.

So when Allowance, Capulet-optioned, buff brace that always stood
topple, thinly rhymed families, replete, to never come again, implore,
exhaust summoned; equip, abundant in gaffs, ran-to-outwit,
taxing Napp under catalogue's cheat, so crime –
the always God-tree exposed – could, those usual purpose.

Shiny suits plenty bags embrace, twin beams thump.
And some would have: on to the zoo! or zero; kept track of who.
But saddlebacked on stupor and a-snide trim, tried an audience.
There topic drop, occupy, Staff and rod many rulers resultant fastened–
so all the thinking ones in guise, haste and giddy, the dire
group problem were really not upon. So a past, going-nowhere,
for cheery good time, it's all there! cereal box read, llm game face,
soda fret with tragic final finish hooked, and bummed again.
Which despite, a few would hike `round; sit alley with some;
camp materially last ontologic bother till the fairly come.
As recur, a burger a mcdonald's became, a sears tooled to sleep,
pretty penny's, some; while slights did merciless, the people among;
and christian with mates to that late race did succumb.

Petty-in-the-pants, editioned, would still dehorn thunder beasts;
smash bother ant; rail crazy sufficient to not suffice.
But cut, paste could retouch blue, red skies, and wide and long
middling mind get airy theory to compile adrift, or aplomb
comply, as if there was brilliance, as if brilliance could live there.   101

As if quiet taint - expressionless, wordful concomit, electron/positron;
scrappy in scrum with mighty bristle rack and sea baying riotous
sun against - could send gifts to a blissful rock planet
where God and Justice, soooo-many ton'd, weighed all scales: off!

In the almost air they agreed then, they were outrivaled! That
present in the breathe, the It! The I! doesn't know WTF is going on!...
So, they bailed a tear for man and his shank, shredding hand
that leaves kin Earth a doom of sand...and said to one another
t he bubbly clouds, aren't so much anymore!
t here may be something in it for you;
t ake something with you when you go!...

TWO PHILOSOPHERS AT THEIR RHETORIC

Row academy! Friend and culprit yet.
For God's adepts, ever in number, should come up to His, One.
Should be cautious on those waters, though magnificent, what!

The one's cost to realize, exceeding, yet
easier in fulfill than the other was - *Why* should, very useful,
around *What* grow for reverence and furtherance spies!

Survive of who would tame shine-in-reverie to save safe, she Earth!
For Love and the allure of men in her God-strain sees who and what is.
The adore of Interventions for the other with stare and hair-pull,

showed how to engage, as individual, without surrender to any
of society's restraints. The moral agenda seeing affinities-between, in,
added right-action, each his political and personal stake.

The exchange of the like of man, deft in extension, shares to extend,

tries to believe in one-part the having, even if miniature,
of the also beneficent attributes ascribed to Him.

Lest the abnegate, self- sabotage, de-human and-other-charge alienate
sell as self-canceling puffed up part; like the glorifying of the light sort
bill-banded and blues handed over others, media-ly.

That indeed! sends mapper to overall settle his blank eases
on the rich scarcity he leases, of thoughten-change
in and on the strain of doubt, others falsely swallow,

to fill needs-filling and run raggedy-anns ragged,
lay outers to inners among the flowers and grass
in wave-eye of the isn't that's played the all.

So that let be! Pelf is currency and curse.
Whereby, 'over against' vulgarity, the one could
Method in its 'look at me!' through a window, high, cast.

And agreed round they, not abandoning dead duff,
rights-basic all should for everyone wake.
Which head-high controls from the quick and deliver! Love!

Requests, abhorrent, constrained by no civil duitical bind,
they gave of what is owed the smallest from the largest
and battle's never-delight, unfolded on the floor of balance.

Note: Prof. Cornel West. & Prof. Roberto Mangabeira Unger.

HIGH ASTRONOMY (Universe of Discourse)

Cosmos – 23rd
Quadrant – Alias Life
Universe – 474978,322,000901,000,000,000,000,000,000

Galaxy – Milk Way
Star Cluster – Perviant
Star – Large Dumbo
Planet – 3rd from its Star
Atmosphere – Un-livable
Surface – Un-livable
Life – Cellular
Domain – Eukaryote
Kingdom – Animalia
Phylum – Vertebrate
Class – Mammalia
Order – Primate
Family – Hominidae
Tribe – Hominini
Genus – Homo
Species – Homo Sapien, Sapiens
        Prosecutor(s) – Remaining Universes!
        Indicted – UoD of inhabitants!
        Verdict – A waste!
        Sentence – Abandonment! - Abandoned!

TWO TO THREE NAOMIS (At Their Windows)

How control minimizes
as we all die guilty of some offense.
Gray windows fence the case went to court with.
Attractiveness is the behavioral goal that slips.

Gratitude is in her East.
Humility, West.
Grace dawdles the pastures Nor
and Reverence swamps South.

Huh! And that's the rough aspiration!
in the come and go a default is.
Daunt life lets, soothes, does even the mortal world plague
still rose-windows against.

A place for the entertainment set,
lunch comes, goes; duty rises, falls in all Comptons,
dells of Chino or Paris, canyons of New York.
Every rule except maneuver restricts to get away with.

A flake on clever window
and one in clear heart rail, if clement valence.
But what is that to one, in their march
that wants the shortest of outcomes, shortcuts?

There it is! It's all there in time!
The smile of abundance, wrench of success. Slow walked
the older in their history in the room when love died,
and nothing said, but Superheroes were expiring; Dear be that!

Kitchen-in against that backdrop, seated by the door, her shop,
Mother taking names and giving numbers,

warehousing the impossible and for tries cries.
Two to three Naomis, reticulating lives.

Notes: Valence: degree of attractiveness toward a behavioral goal. Turbid: confused; muddy, foul, etc. Reticulate: resembling a net; having veins, fibres or lines crossing (a leaf); to divide, mark or construct so as to form a network; to become reticulated. My Mother, Grand-Niece, and Allen Ginsberg's Mother. Compton, Ca; Compton-Verney, Warwickshire, England, etc.

THE DESERVING KIND

At reads now,
but play for a woman, raw and upset by wiles
he knows not how to fend, save absence -
so, urge Falcon intent, soar above said intense.

Man, a grape her vine, unsettle,
be a care left minus better.
His arms collapse.
That soft voice of welcome saps
whole reason, extracts prong, disarm-es.

Seed then speechless as he is to fish-giving waters.
Prepare kind earth, when the root-deep-claw alters.
For none have right to
what kills glee earth.

Slight respect won't fill Idris' provident ant horn,
when he slumbers through amber dawn;
whose radiant days rarely burst
settled-with cement off cold, gray trench; types' together worth.

And listen! He to every worry does not start.   106

Strong! bursts perceiving heart.
Compulsion made comfort's key
counts success, names these
in cries of faring better.

Rack through shield disquiet, myriad helpless have gone
greet the timeless dimple. Back at her seat, plow, pond
doused biological imperative glances the many
irks and pucelage worn in her perfect ken gone or having come.

I DIED A LITTLE THAT DAY

when Cain did Able. Since then none have been
to take away the stain from that hand of man.
I died when the first one said, chop it down and they did
for warmth or other, leaving only badlands, spoil for yonder.

I died when Muse African Pharaohs tried
lighter complex to civilize. Too much mirror?
What did they do - Egypt, Phoenician, Greek, Roman etc.
with it? Well, look around. This could all be earth nature,
not tamed; honoured in its leave be and let lie,
to larger extent we pray by.

I died when we were unable our air to franchise basic;
some once highflyer, down from there
kicked a lot `a nasty about, blast away the not now
with something to burn, ladies and gents.

I died not staying on track, and *not*! from doing so.
I died when they broke Urias; when Abraham was willing,
when Lao Tzu, Zola, any Greek, Roman robed white

toured sell-fish render, had a city to leave,
or John or Peter, Jill, Jane. Yeah, any Joey Mombo

because they spoke against the not Just, that thing
All men, women everywhere know; not by science
wave handing particles like throws Frisbee in the what medium...
Albert! Albert! Albert? Wake up... but straight on
like The Halls at Luxor and everywhere else for True strive.

I shied when that king did that thing at Kheta,
abandoned to overman. When every Outpourer of life,
name of God! Horus! accomplished what they did then,
among poor do-able, die-able man.

When fish of the mountain, goats, each used live item are food to them.
When every poet or philosopher run out of family bears that; I cry.

When Arjuna, self-seeking preservant, god-poked, had to decide
I cried when Herakles killed his children god-stoked;
when Gilgamesh coming along, had to unlearn childhood, I think,
when poet Plato laid high praise aside, flogging merciless good Homer,
who, from Aesop only brought Lady Literature.

I died when men and women of no learning crucified Jesus The Christ.
When that poor youngster or innocent down south was massacred,
when Shaka Or Geronimo had to Zulu un-nerving Europeans, I died,
when they sent away those Dark who, courageous as always,
saved The Church, when they let Bulls claim `lifeless', full pastures,
when bullying cowed Galileo, murdered Bruno, Joan, et al again!
So many other human feeler, and all those not-witches Mom, I died!

Pictures, descriptions, like Pop's, about Michel-Ange's work, though,
on The Chapel and much more he'd seen as Liberator I liked
when sun deigned to shine on my poor soul and I some truth bold;   108

happy to expose destruction; always in mountains mostly
when a new piece of writing broke veil!
Happy you worked at The Five-side during the war Mom still!

Happy when rain, not too cold or frozen hit face,
when some musician set some part a pace, or almost any poet drool.

I cried when white boys hated us. When Mom and Dad after Mass,
drove their rug-rats to museums or the miles of orange groves it was Love!
Then, happy again when Bunyan Vanity Fair'd,
when Shakespeare tried what Drake brought back;

when my girls were taken care of, safe in his own safe Home.
Happy! When Browning wrote Why He Was a Liberal, and Emerson
and Thoreau were born. I cried a little when teenage Rousseau
was locked out of Zurich, even more when he wouldn't fess up.
When Carlyle (liked for much his philosophy, and more for Goethe proximity)
joined - off the reservation, and when they went devil on all those Indigenous

I died when Villon in *his* way left the reservation, when Wordsworth was
belittled by Byron; and worried incessant, for high-flying, human Coleridge,
and when Carlyle couldn't be convinced.
I cried a little when Joyce finished Ulysses. But when Finnigan hit the Wake,
dense harvest words plied owning, maybe pretentious at Einstein's theories
I shied a little.

I cried when Proust wouldn't stop, when reading how Tolstoy
from his station never came out,
and when Dickinson couldn't leave the house, being woman.
I died when Fanon sickened, when Socrates, Pericles, DuBois,
as those above, were to-leave by the gathered, asked, even as
one does what work one does, for the best, toiling; Oh sacrifice!

When Gandhi though prejudice, any woman, both Johns, Martin,   109

Bobby, Malcolm, any number innocent or near innocent were made mess of
I died when Toussaint was deceived, regular deceivers offering their gear:
the ghastly lie, on that stone there with him, I died,
when stealing, because could his fire, they un-boated Garvey,
laying aside all the African Humanitarian immaculate despoiled,
who now are us, though now pardoned.
I died when the `n' word was flung from anywhere!
   I kept my mouth shut never, at least I hope I did that.

FULL OF CAKE

A branch would at slightest alarm cave.
A quite stellar oppression, a quit stellar acceptance,
   for racial redirect, un-sharp corner, for a rondeau or a coin.

And grave to-them initiative that they duty clad,
perceived duty full, was at retention left,
induced unhappinesses of injustices' tear,
   having the new millennia to wear.

Catholic Dictionary Volume VIII (1910) New York:
"...He is the father of Christian chronology. Little is known of his life
and little remains of his works. He is important chiefly...
his influence on Eusebius...all the later writers of Church history
among the Fathers, and on the whole Greek school of chroniclers.

His name, 'Julius Africanus' says that he was an African;
Suidas calls him "a Libyan philosopher""
then goes on the article to attest their disbelief in tortured expositions;
betrothed racial superiority, gunning-the-engine claims;
to detest, un chart, ignore feats African.

110

Thus gash of indifference: one that wants the worlds'
on-these-disturbances-of-privilege of access away from,
thrown like child that for a candy to a parent falsifying,
has its very self drunk deep the intolerance,
    destruction of why of inevitable defeat.

Titus I: 16. "They profess that they know God;
but in works they deny him,
being disgusting/abominable, and disobedient,
and toward ever good work discredited/reprobate."

Here one would not from a storm into a storm usually cape,
advise more common sense dig upon a high ground,
or portion a branch to ones' own hug. Is it a branch or part the thing?

One does knaw the bit, in a vision perfect nevertheless,
Joy in happenstance, run to emergency, cope with,
embrace and translate that day of men and angels
when with His winning drops in.

PLEASANT CHILL

African, 'Indies, Persian, Greek and else hind,
scare-up library's natter, go the safe end to play.
And that will do young man! wheezes into a speakers louden
and horn "Gotta sort out this Geezer, yeah!?" cries through
a sleeve that's torn. In it, Gorman came over low saw-tooths,
up, down Bear State's north south routes;
so chowed the dogs how! Sleuth, wrestler;
all slower-to-get brakes it well out a' there.
You know, the knoll Nile sharing, society and 'friendly' neighbor?
chances mound that all Matter excavated appear white somehow.
Bids but two of any and - bungles with the registers,
which is good's extricate embarrassed by usurpers embarrassed trowel.
Or, if sweaty byproduct's streaming, and won't stop,
it's baths theatre, and Text the barber!
Tents can't leave! America's at Fitzgerald's gate.
Who have yet to read; though, today's lines claim Frostian.
And there the favored fevered example's truths unfollowed,
want to think poets' ouveures over, and "Are we there yet?" their drivers.
But they're probably not.

Note: Natter: chatter, etc. Idle talk or conversation.

¿À LA SAINTETÉ?

Movement on beliefs would not,
excitement caterer breed difference in,
those void-less when, printempts obtient tout rompy
dans la forêt, Été en contact avec soi puant;
a content-is-king chanson, where prophets feared,
Possibility dropped, while broad, the poet,
practiced flights impractical, and
held Responsibility High under tuck arm...
   Decision indecision active specifics late and older
ages cross, scold The rapidity of rivers, their either sides,
flotsam on gurgle's caught-lurch. But that these
license accept as license got like you of verse,
from hunch, from God, whose lot! Is certain.

Thence Evening balm a scratch curve,
rub good dull to good calm nerve; a word!
  Love, self-seducer of wants; Love that knows a How,
bright before best things in best seasons;
bow not as suppliant sold bobble pitch, or troyed
only by but tradition,   where Goodness comes
with intention as would crouch a crowd; as best Use,
principled child, sealed on delivery-day side;
shouldering unions honest men, and wares – self to defend,
  un-furl, so minus solid rock!
Else evidemment (nothing is longer crossed. Not swords, stars,
rocks, nor rifles) vous êtes là et je suis ici;
  as sanctity tormenting every shore confesses every sea.

Notes: To Sanctity? Printempts...Spring gets all rompy in the forest. Eté en...Summer in touch with stinky self. Evidemment: obviously. You are there, and I am here.

113

"STILL ALIVE!"

De Musset to Baronne Dudevant
and the Italian doctor in that movie.
Me to you who fib this rock;
je suis la! nature not amused;
WCW to his wife and reviewer;
- dirigible last with screens' slow debris
in blood for stroke and heart attack,
while words of cheer reward effort
(he's seventy-nine then)
in peninsular and land-locked hands
that bore word-good doctor over transom.

For him, between worlds, acompany baffle and tickle
immortal might run a while.
The dying if/when, page-turn again - memory
in men's hearts, gain their tongues,
should 'Solid house' the wife's, 'variable foot' his,
in sheath and conscience lift, griefs' soil,
and cloak shrugs fall in completion.
 The rest? Life's Less,
count frays spread-wreck guiltless suns.

Oar, if they learn, constant like him,
and split hying the medium,
tracked now and in some future Desire;
sessile will pay Providence braile through abuse;
lead How, Where, When and Why
to list-significance of Who, and turnaround.
    But if you're alone get a mirror! And grow.
    Because as age everything and nothing
    like hug mistake laughs follow, just such embri;
    but that, has a Pass sign over.   114

And society breathing feels? May they go deep to rescue you!

Notes: Je suis la: I am here! Re: William Carlos Williams' (and his wife's) interview in The Paris Review1962, POETRY NO. 6. Sessile: permanently attached or established; not free to move about. Braile: a rope used to haul a sail up or in; a dip net in which fish are hauled aboard a boat; to hoist, etc.

FROM INDEPENDENCE MANLINESS PROSPERS

In bunt of meaning mind, you borrowed a vortex, cone,

pyramid, as from forest, as usual tower, start.

Vegetable geometries formed an isle

in a summerless sun-on winter style.

Contemplate ate itself,

as duplicitous on neither host exceled,

and amphiboly for either shore dared,

'Take the work out!'

Ahead, fine feel Stop & Explore

of an Androcles' vital for his lion

did wed not-tense the terse-trending tyrant,

tide-tackling toadant, action is.

And as world's a wide field and everyone attendant,

there's Teddy Afro, maybe Sir or `Ma-Lady Dancealot,

or Johnny Anything-but-simple who oils Earth's rot,

great Nature, its proper spot.

Awkward higher thrusts the one, votary to souls' not having done.

Other, to a wildland's scarce tracks, desperation in from hot, lost end;

Apollo after Diane, thing in spin;

 gold leaf on shelves Sitzende Frau corrade!   115

Then, he her trounce, she his '...for the blond pussy too late!'

At home they rarely played or prayed, said;

as noring, the sons of panarchy plied panic without.

The margin was too narrow to contain it, stayed a straining Fermat.

And There is Amiri something in the way of things!

Still, in the signaldom, you'll be found in the coming hour

because just now in sun's past-meridian a limb seems a familiar river,

and does cause last year's leaves ambitions fragile shiver!

Notes: Amphiboly: sentence or phrase susceptible of more than one interpretation. Androcles: an enslaved person who removed a thorn earlier from a lion's paw, that later spared him in the arena. Sitzende Frau: Henri Matisse. 'The blonde...' Charles Bukowski. Pierre de Fermat's last theorem. Poet Amiri Baraka.

THE LADY, THE DEEP AND ATLAS

"On every ear the oft told drama lands an apprehension.
But I will tell as in this strange corridor you and I, and these others sit,
that in a time that seems apparition, in die dagen,
in the land of birth – and I may soon stand! –
emerald consent for the herds, their grasses;
sunrise glow for the inhabitants, their glory - I was a king's daughter,
scion of Gracious III, a good, elding, and saint-like man.
  Not much land, though some working on.
- And pet-smile me not a Syrinx, I had many a suitor.
But authority was my bare; and better metatragedy Hecuba didn't!

 "In that land then, where rank is first, all feeling parts take shorter arcs.
Indeed, when occasion smiled, and rich sand beaches were at naked feet;
the blue-haired ruler of Everdeep, made approaches my ladiness
to take and for himself, in some far lowly, surely wet to forever keep.
Call it - when in dissent I more and more refused; high wave, loud crash,
like as if the poor creature had never been denied, as I suspect hadn't,
 from every quarter of his authority came un-pleasant on.

"But I, in fulfill gnothi seauton, added those quotient –
buff mendicant; and rallied clear. Still, many hearing of the bout,
even in reaches at distance, at recite these engages, scatter.
Then horde the-worst that overtook came. That soothe our
(that other high court) convictions that each knows marks em ---,
but that – only stand mild, smile-filled evenings
through wine-dark eyes' can correct.
Like one of your Catholic Counsel's deep imperatives
to matter Europe; a joke; the wee city and its bank; of walls of streets
leading, oh congruent sculpt! Cul-de-sac collides! only to harms and ruin.
So that every story clipped ancient! Come gamble in hot leaps
and with chance abound in the abodes of them are empaneled.
For normal ones, to their Beatitudes, knowing the safe way,

volition's lights..." she added, "glared!"

Just then, with strong back, and meaning; aside; the open gate holding,
a burly one no one noticed, head, from the load, pointing down, laid;
"But on your own?" And adjusting momentarily to comfort his lift,
that weight of a whole world he had collect and eager'd,
that world that seemed like the mortal of an elegy,
kept mysterious for a short time more in the air up,
gravitytime pursued, most surely seemed glad,
   of those present, at the affair.

"And we thought of the issue as fetch not wretch," he carried on,
"certainly not wrench as a Saul or Odysseus might, for disgrace.
But also as dances to Life strained Watch, if even therehere
through God's dark and lowly night. So a mild few years ahead
you may or may not empty into inhospitable. De-max the years
and the cases for many centuries after." Burly continued,
"The subjective and negative optative giving over to optimal
screed skills: silent walks with the services you'd render –
So, scoff not, but tip of hat, be that!

"Standard welcomes that land on planes that shift Nature apocalyp
get all they need of mixture in on!" He was thought to finish.
  Then like a recalled fog back to sea, at high-speed vacuumed, almost red shift,
disappearing, "...but you spoiled all thaaattt!" came entwining,
vortex going-to-line somehow back, from a very far off, as last gasp to ear, mind.

   Note: In die dagen = [Dutch] In those days.

IN PHILOSOPHY'S ROOMS

With morning wake sacked,
telling export explore of Deceit kept
over stroke and cold mattress
through gale
`till alms of day could better board and badger.

Only possible of Just, in light armour,
afoul fools' hustling detinue
continued glance and pleased
aboard aubade's red yellows,
wise to action right, there.

 Enough so any logic not cut at hips,
while he did not sleep – such rights
as sense and reason get - might arrive
long siesta of non-guilt, treasure of the Just,
until even those robbed might flesh it.

Flair bend, go-about in philosophy's rooms
on muster of minds gone, despite additions here,
agreed sums there, that some may know
Feel sits summit of affairs. Miss and hit
and what's-it-all-for center in the civil garden still, to escape it.

And Ocean Stream storied, once ancient, neglect,
was smile, giggle aside and not that drink
that surrounded super continents?
How far do memories go?
  Master Feel, Dream People, still proof the calculi.

Notes: Detinue: detention (unlawful) of something due, etc. Aubade: a poem or song
of or to the morning, etc.

IN THE STREAM

Twenty-one thousand in and thin intends to sand
a harvest on drought.

Now numbered, days taught tears in vita's stream,
from clearing heave, 9 or no.

Torque stout used of figure-out, watch
the whys and whats of humane behavior!

Don't mean to hum, no, nor sing Montanist answers out
like many to cruise

but life seems like Solomon: 'personal, said,
 'more than (we) knew.'
Each genuflect, long last, wobbles cribs within,
knowing comfit route.

Thus, from no visits the why we were, and He is,
never free, see? Stop pouring doubt.

Notes: 365 days/yr. X 59 yrs. = 21,535 days. Montanist: adherent to a 'Christian' sect
arising in the late second century stressing apocalyptic expectations, the continuing
prophetic gifts of the spirit, and strict ascetic discipline.

JOUST

The lists, revised!
All are barbed to survive
bawd men of war
who will not starve sore tragedy.
Make friend of hate
in treble blind
if you've no mind.
You can't withdraw
can't stay
but neither will be left behind.
In another's confused state,
see you do not lull from 'one and same is all,'
clutching difference in that fall.

INCOMING (OR Vignette of a god's son)

Pascal, Mozart, Heidegger a few wisdoms to lend.
Hefty Delacroix, Mr. J.M.W. Turner and combative Whistler
Arts' outgo. Yet hangs the question: how do bore
to incomplete exhaustion `till kind of heel?
Scholars of old lifted/were handed Old Black magics.
But some, led trusty tend, to pillage, war, rape, theft of herds
to get by. Horses – careful yet – slower, wider, further
halt-mannerisms to hand, may wield momentarily to go fast,
overlay in rash the wreath of ZE Ever-Present.
But you! At that flat, toiled sun, must speak peace among!

Thereat, having spoken, and the union of two sides,
count weirs with em! There, 'Natus homo est!
All, with men clothed, Earth experiences hells a-million.

That lovely get-along of all things, un-gathered in the prior formless,
now within their determined bounds, and traveled far
from good gantry Gold Rule of stern Saturn, to less shining times
with trumpets of straight, sword and helmet; of the evil burst
of the age of hard iron, whence came war which,' Ovid continues,
'fights with both iron and gold... where sons inquire
into their fathers' years before the time; piety lies vanquished;
the last of the immortals abandons blood-soaked earth,
from whence fled modesty, truth and faith; and those sons of blood,
following the Giants, have angered High Heaven Host.'

'Yet, rightly cautious of the strength in possibles of fire, The Thunderer
lays aside cisbolt and on the winds and rushing steeds of water calls
till, "nos duo turba sumus...we too are the throng," "turbulence total"
eared by Pyrrha, is exhaled by Deucalion. And those two have
the goddesses' advice to interpret; stones to bones
 new men and women devise; while the story goes,   122

moisture and heat produce all other and each living thing.'

Finally, well-wishing and brief; young men, of the two alive that interval,
Phaethon, in wish to show an all without what he owned he was,
son of a god, asks far too much, is not mature by much,
and ether's not there scorches; friction skalds and with the stick of God
scratches the whole move-as-fast-as-can getup, fit for fire;
that horse, trace, chariot, all! wide scattered for far-flung pickup.
 And though 'he greatly failed, he more greatly dared'
   they etched on his stone.' Epitaph for good men.

   Notes: "natus homo est," born man is ("Then man was/is born"): Ovid: Bk 1; 78, and
   most within the half-quotes belongs to Ovid, Metamorphoses: Bk 1. I'll revel if he'll
   forgive my painting on his old, yet still novel, canvas.

      HONEST

Tired. But grit as hadn't felt that.
Smile routine, prize its chore, copes examination:
that some, will rise
to command worse hierophants to ground.

Iterance, sound praise, and days ounce,
a post: unfellowed illum,
alone and hope strong in practice,
half the man would without
should snark shark overall art cast
as fashions' un-Goding, less;
to rise in Creation gratios, unguarded.
Cymbal'd and drummed, schmaltz
first-rights record how
rung-alarms court advance.
We have the many gone past-attired

to rolfed, charged entry, for who could afford.
  Sorry! Sad, unforgive, crumpled paper!

And jip-noonists who rob sack of night,
call it peril, bugbear, dis-tender, out-elegant,
roll of nothing without, have lit the confusion.
List now Italian Dubliner word hordest who
entire romp sindark nave followed blindest; and
'hold (his) mind (the fool apparently) were she an Ethiope,'
shaved.   I skip. You wave. Gall cleave,
prepare dry spirit stone soon theing;
show suit trouser teams in return
thir flying-off of care in Confessions (Je vous salue!) memoried
for man's best deeds.

But now des rochers, des arbres,
de monceaux de pierres consacrés par ces actes,
blink in chaotication, and form tech Choose saying
  resign the evening's work. So do.

Notes: Hierophant: priest in ancient Greece, expositor, advocate. Unfellowed, sindark nave: J. Joyce. Alone and...Amiri Baraka. Schmaltz: sentimentality, etc. Rolf, rolfing (1970): method of muscle therapy for the physical and emotional self. "The rocks, the trees, the piles of consecrated stones by their acts..."

OTHER WORLDS

It would be necessary to hammer selves home
to beef up malcontent. Service is a dire, but desired state.
We shall our part. Missions are not by our kind failed.
 We have tasted broth the nectar of passing years.
Our service in degrees have beyond the seven-fold gone.

It will not do to act harm; we have sights on us.
Our release of potent has more. Single will turn from, to many times.
And the pain, in our aim be twice prime resemblance.
New forms of Patience and Forgiveness will the cool air affair.
Disillusion, like reign regency, out of respect, will never
by our illusion be strung along. None, under our care will, rabid,
chief justice fail.   And necessaire, that strain was scarce of,
with the plain evidence of return will not sit ranging with the fruit in concourse
and warm blanket wrapped patent, over views of the halt destruction
and meanness at rest aside a tend fire, passing all in stolen quiet
    in these the winters of our descent.

So that neither moon, planet, nor star will indict and justice starve
at our black holes' table where only the foolhardy, hole-for-spout,
tempests braking, pulled through lengthy, parched horizons,
stretched till nothing but the weir sound of empty's fulness
and Dames said to be certain, aware the ride of spiral's chiral recursant,
will be found.
But there grow sequence, pull tight the fulling year, and like pieces on a grid,
close-confident, glory tight, fair speak but plain language each to each
    in this our containment.

- IN THE PRESENCE -

Case of disbeliefs. How cured, a Compton man finding himself
in the wood of holly; not magnificently outstretched low-land
west wind would brush of an evening; holy uprise, prime's perfect angle
and the wood due worship? I asked in spirit of relief if it was too soon
to prize happy poems. Always is there room for happiness! came back.
in success of vital habit, eye or arms' embrace,
chance smile set crown a face, in gladden nature's crafted place!

Truly, in heat of Former fan flame. Wood, now history shriek shiver to aim!
Swift her color does Day bring misery with her mystery.
Unlearned knowledge trains retreat, takes slack;
no care, zealot, with basic warnings grin, haggard back!
Wisdom, confident laments – boards ale, illusion, fear of other,
erasure, denial, trove as fray of fun and laughter!
Duty, vision, future, stand dock for question,
only feudal bother find, `cause there rail the simpleton!

In high menace, Olympe de Gouges and women-many,
their names herstory rather, threw tentative aground going,
and Penance let the rest, eat their superior and them ravage,
by autre men of opinion old, who treated selves guests,
on a no-guest planet; so that Time, ready in fragiles to mount
with history to sue for freedoms, scurry for detail strove;
and led the baleful, to runnel with words, being
armours' enhance, no harrow!   I was confused; wood continued.

Now new hour, honkin` big raindrops from ghostly cloud rip, severe.
Flood, no water, and torrents of plastic run out rears.
Among discards, again! with doer, Desire; to all her wonders married;
paint reality with tell light that falls in shadow; and know for the first,
there is no place safer than mind, that least safe place of all;
as a phlegmyton, take another hit for the winter team;

and wave of treetop to wind stay a sea at that level!

In vie torment, in gazes' amaze, responsibility tried, teamed,
let day go willing on; having "treated all, like for self want;" in worship
'touched earth, and scattered it on your chest,' as we, for awe, for guard;
never recon old, washed or newbie controlly drubbed,
in a weird fling falling furthest; never gall in a passe or rave
break-in rude who do diablo dearest, and we will fend for you!

` Cause not many before got much of a lead! That few did,
hide ruthless bind of pet peeves has; point whole missed, and –
they have our sympathies, but attentions too; that may have need a while
Sampson trust, Herculean sheen, Serapis full-at-all-points as sharpens,
that will not be too much, nor please!

For victory-reared nonstop was always keep watch, tote bale,
lift valiant life after in-moment happening with the Without.
And a-tide aggression's pockets, each succession's success Great `G&R!'
and nothing less seems. Where hardship and persevere own reach and reward;
where there are corrects-up, proper guards, participates; wood did fend for you!
 and droit deer shy cud in the yard!

Notes: 'touched earth...' and G&R -(Golden Rule), among others = inscription on stella of
King Neferhotep, 1730 BC: "The reward of the man who does is what is done to him: in the
heart of God, this is Maat." - Intro, Note 13 and/from The Tale Of Sinuhe; R.B. Parkinson
trans.; Oxford U. Press © 1997. Droit \drwä; a legal right.

WARY

He with himself was as wary as he with others.
'Custer died for your sins' – the ditty goes.
But wrath idiota learns not if he wins.
Spoiled furthest, a fen wind, a spend send to soil if uninitiate.
   Agenda items on the tenth were taken.
Each month dressed for 'two-backed' concourse;
smiles furlongs breathed across his current sunk chest,
in tendence to upset the fair.

A desert of man would scratch Her turf
his sot-hunted hundred hands.
But she with Between Things elopes first,
their dowry, per alloi, each the other
vie to trump the distant direction
and shake tinsel-like the speed taken to get there, here,
that place, once.

FOUR

IS LOVE BORN

But perhaps in kind book of change,
brow ill disaster by disbelief close hatched,
fainting hopper of higher will,
sacred emerald of sameness lost.

Before mighty shears declined, reduced phalanx
hind hearts on tender fed;
where all the world was temn to find
logic's color, separation's need.

Cool feel on better days
hail no need to good its cheer,
a morrow upend.
Might soon, under injury, cope with feet there.

So, going, remember Love.
This ink of kindness
ever always, always was
ever its own best option.

Huddled, discovered cheated man,
undone of heavens' gatemen; rude cursing hatreds
leans languid side casement still.

Rock down were made to go.
And with such time gone,
corruption glowers its greed toll, moldings to a tizzy,
silent the way of unseen stone roll,

as others' blinking decades car'd fast -
sinkhole stunned, were found witless cubs aghast,
who did not follow mother. But you, moan on! down-light will!

Tomorrow you'll aside a little! And that might pay the bill!

Notes: Temn: fr. L. temnere to despise.

WHEN THEY CRY

Modified by feel, point and process of contact, ≥ 1,
even cozy old guard, destructor of species,
from stolid raise, heel fear at totter,
will choke, steel, follow barrel chest in heaves;
untether salty drop that slaps surprised surface.

Women and children with the man quiver, nothing is safe;
animals whimper, there is a shaking cold, the drip misgiving,
dame chance summoned, drags grumble denial Sparta
by grumble denial collar, `till H too and some O restored! deliver.
And sunk – 'Hush Now! Don't you cry!' hot breath, emptor,
cornering the market, dives to recall bottom. His book of spells fired,
no one trick pried, manhood revivified, a hundred
and ten lies drench; to his chin mired.

Meanwhile masculine clay unbound, less divide, finds in weep,
vessel filling, a relief to limp to. Dams brake; water filed world with, on.
Love a-branch the pain of injustice by justice filters.
'Relating with dis-relates' has jumped Poetics' stick,
drawn fool and hero, warm holds of nature sweep in.

Still, veiled ardour for 'illegal, immoral gains, political crimes,'
proofed by tears batters; blame Herakles for in-house rampage;
in myth, he upset that god. The Ithacan himself let men insult divines,
whipped that poor poet, and would un-free women attack for indenture.

Bough, note, you hang in a fog, like a picture stuck on a wall;
` till affordance of patience
gets another thing done and reclaims the sodden hall.

VISIONS OF APOCALYPSE

1.   MELTING
Sometimes the World ascents to answer our questions.
Others, knowing we have the answers
or equipment there for, leaves half-blind,
 half-wondering, but never denied.
    I sat at the peak of a roost wondering,
    sometimes into doff silence,
    with words that shook the tranquil.
    It was not needed. They knew what they were
    and what was necessary.
Some took part, some took it apart. Shocked Wood
whirred somewhere and distinctions either hid
like the guilty, jumped around huff some,
or after pulled hide and jump, for the dust, could find no sun.
    It was alright. One house bigger, we had our pleasures,
tweaks and non-observances that fed the non-health.
I would have thought every being could see
where in fact we were. But I see now,
there was a lot of not looking.
Understanding had long thrown itself in, over,
as your boarding might allow. Such that kith
claimed whim, and kin – nowhere to be found
in the madden. I sank again as I sang. And the fire was hot.

2.   TOODLE DO
"The high Voltage is my sinecure." the one to the others.

I don't know what I saw in that dream,
But it could not be named nice.
They, on the power lines, brought, I think,
by tinge frequent hum, were not from my world.
Danger ranged in their tries.

I thought, why far from Innocent Charter of Childhood,
under volume collapse, virus/non-appetite/hot day
and hooter night should I be given such a view?
Was it a movie I'd seen come unbidden
to ride understanding, oblivion remanding?
Surely it was no gift of vision a deserver is given.
So what the F was it?

3.   TREE
God bless. It's Wednesday, my assigned day to water
between 6:00 and 10:00 am, and you got that.
- Trash was again taken. Post Office, after key to lock,
the mails coughed. I paid the bills, voted, signed my ballot,
and left where told.

It may be of excellent merit and beneficial
to strike the personal/singular, like a tad addict,
from your writing.   But the impersonal,
with many another high deceit/wrong eye -
the Robert Lowell elide - may have brought us here.
I wonder how much I've given, and how much done without.

4.   MOTHER MARY
Thrown Heiddy. No! more droplet street-scene dropped
into moment's parti-colors gaiety. Then police abuse,
sinister smoke, gas chaotic,
and the half-good man was pressing Her into my hands.
  Her eyes were real. Her hands feel I.... could,   133

like looking into those eyes, never describe.
Panicked runs, the hack and drag of child,
   people fall.   I ask, pulling, if she could run. We did.
  She got ahead of me and fell badly.
  I went to gather...   too vulnerable to be real!
But not a hint of anguish. Her Goodness was everything
passing through me, and anything would have been done
to protect Her.   A little more proairetikos
  and the half-good man was there again.
Did we make the rendezvous? Was there one?
  She was broken.   I woke up.

Notes: Volume collapse = Earthquake. Heiddy: 'affectionate' as said, for Heidegger.
Pro(h)airetikos (inclined to prefer, purposive; will) – see Aristotle's pro(h)airesis (choice,
purpose, resolution, etc.).

    VIS MEDIACATRIX

  Up where trail becomes a seep because it can and
  alp waives it so,
  we follow old bend-gain on arrivals,
  illicit in turns and roll and gain by hush and flush,
  tie-tossed shoe quotes from μήτηρ pines' help rush.

  Read lands on what bears with;
  forest un-washed in catkin eye kiss;
  Knowing Dealt from Knowing Done;
  heart for extravagance, or
  Go With It to You Must Not!

  At inner-wellness,
  teaching by exertion caught,
  hurst and earth and women and men   134

have met, unrelent in concourse -
bowsprit bristlecone brought by -
as designate our badly shaded day camp.

Then dolmen weathered
bedrock; fine-tuned scar, project!
on that peak, lull akin round stone! And like
in all Love's stories, with softly minds and solemn part,
take again, the wild, smile-tinged treatment for the heart.

Notes: Vis mediacatrix: force, power of medicine – treatment, etc. Hurst: OE hyrst; a wood;
grove; wooded eminence; undergrowth, etc. Bowsprit: a projecting member over the bow of
a ship. Dolmen: tabletop-shaped tombs, ancient, found throughout Europe.

FOLK TUNE
  ala Joseph Brodsky

In freefall from calling up;
in punishment desecration to shut.
Smart sitting malcontents who fracked last
loll wheelchairs ahead in petty cash.

Nor does desert make-up for soil gone bust
nor last trees replacements diverse enough.
And exercise, unaccustomed to stretch, extend,
rest of body little healing will lend.

Are you warm little man in your monkey suit,
in shoes traveled farther than you,
when like bottled water from farthest reach
you've come to the table a dry relief?

You'll note your eye, its coupled squint,

135

in strain to follow where season went.
Bleak furled flag of corporate privates;
fallow the field, those moneyed pirates!

And if unrest is response with honour
and were left loves with the family farmer;
was to settle better Dantons, Madibas forward!
Bloodless revolutions, from forgiveness onward.

Grown miffed in transfer, about to do,
progeny come to the throne for answers,
whom from the pages of full-coloured story books
Question you, your habit, and ghost glancing around looks.

Notes: Danton: one of the main characters, with more generous feeling for mankind than some in the French Revolution of the late 18th century. Madiba: Nelson Mandela's Xhosa clan name known by.

TESTAMENT II

Coral computer, sweep injury from precious sea floor.
Rotate Death's fertiles - Sprouts mothers' victus chest!
And in this world, one never feels at home anywhere,
  while another is at their hearth everywhere.
Difference, by halt eyes-wide education dare.
Rich-show opposite. Accident and cause determine chance!
Play them there, your spiritual bacchanal, Shyness!

Now every dish, every leftover varietal, one doesn't speak for!
Just note a too-basking serious in the blockchain from one's presence
is not beam to mix much with. But drunk soothe, high-part molder,
pick-em outfit melder, pin to right to life,
survey entangled sources' appellate!
Transfer mandatory at the free-association station.

Light, crook in bend, breakfast petty harms ware.
Name heard, splendid-ways cerebral celebrated, uncamp studious
of that said - poema has and never can a change in things -
 which close examination proves wrong-head deficient.
  What turns then? Do we know unnamed influence
of first encounter with tree waltzing her wind? Was it not a poesy?
Has never Creation, grace on pinion, clear handless arbiter,
there before you, somehow mounted *and* awayed?
 Can such little things be said,
when there is poetry for evidence abroad in nature?

Land disturbances on gilt walls within, that perfection, its blood thin,
must, aside detracts, serve as desireant. Detect too much wine
of compliment and vinegar of opposites it's on/off with, that knows
few large truths, but dash and hopes on same anyway, the trip
to get away with! And may every little truth be a larger truths' heir.
  Note: Victus: [L.], living, food.   137

HIS DILEMMA

War. Innocents must be defended!

War, your hand is too heavy before soft flesh!

War, mad men foment,

cry hate and lie the rest's discontent.

A governing people instead attention sharp

each their obligation to self-governed dreams,

take not part, but full responsibility

for what in name is said, done and meant.

Who, to kill his brother, was he ever right,

whether protective, self-preservation's wary father,

or "We'll have this!" acquisitions' burned-home robber?

Perhaps no answer will fit.

Seeing good men deceived, wrestling souls could,

to favorite son, 'You're not the inheritor by law,

but I'll make you one, if we can fool your brother!'

How now he did not actually say this, but by action,

little faith the one, and jaundiced love the other,

stoop kettle cooked that soup.

And that's where many down-route reality of dichotomies start.

Of good, needing bad to know itself.

      Isn't that wrong! Do, Yeah! miss the point?

And I care not to sun on half-truths aboard such ship.

Nor can "we have no choice!" insistences - every shape and color

easily find a table and beer this hope joint, having pulled a Peliad

 to haste! Says a one to himself.

The point of this, as buff in humble to splay it,

is to beck solution by the-rich-in-love increment.

To maybe, by sweat, eternal effort, land paper love,

folded with in-crease for-them-as-us, each, those other,

on the green of what we have made a peaceful planet.

I know, "What of the evil cannot let stand?"
 Assassination can't answer - it wrong's a wrong within a wrong.
      War can't! That virile spreads unwanted seed
       among the current vanquished.
I fear we'll no answer till each finds love of self in others.
       Which presents as one-part in several mad zillionth of a photon
       in a universe of many, many scads of photons answer!
      But this is where undying faith-in-what-is-right takes over
       for shoddy, mammalian practicality, its wayward materialism.
All elders owe the young and posterity more than the same
broken whys and wherefores, bobbing polluted seas.
The only face to be saved is that of the entire species. Make it, please!

TREE, SWORD AND GRINDSTONE

Colours brighten, a sheen to leaves!
and more than acidic bobbles, the yellow-gold
in Mom and Dad's backyard, those now stopped years,
team of lemon alive, a worrywood, had eyes
a yard, bird, climb and loss of self-hearth not known,
`till cuts with precious blade of the Japanese rite.

Green was an instant of knowing it not
as nurse Failure carried off finish and start.
Hastily, the un-limbered sprint, un-tight grip
dull of sinew saw sword and lemon tree wood
make miss-dent angle the good blade went under.

Now down Freeway, eyebrows to squint Smithy
and honing tool: old curiosity that squat
slept by a watching window on a watching sidewalk.
 Fat two-Pi stone in cart with a wheel that memoried
old automatons encased in class at those old carnies
by the shore, about man high, with wound-up smile and greet,
whose head would sway like a lie side to side,
that were slightly frightening, that one only walked by.

There, await the maker's question on how the ill assault,
push narrow anger that would have plied to manufacture the fault -
Smithy un-genius - as sharpening edge, did saving-face,
and from teeth truth was wrung; ashamed!
And because he seemed hurt by the two or three nicks laid on his work
a promise: to be sure of technique or not cut such at all.
   Better skill purchase first on softer material!
     Years it's been, since that denizen, safed away,
     un-burdened by recall, has breathed free air and thanks!
   All's as it should be; and lives live like that!   140

THE KNIFE EDGE

So many entries of late, embarrass me of myself, but.
This has been my worst terror for a long time:
that we (civilization) had forgotten from whence came
and have 'hacked, cut, fired and racked the growing
green' Gerard Manley Hopkins, and so
under-appreciated nature as to place all on this
knife-edge of destruction.

Hope is that science, spoiled brat's been, with its
Missourian need of proofs, finding those same
proofs exist in felt knowing, has/will rub some of the
heavy sleep from waking eyes, and that
    there's still time to get right.

THE PRINCE

Out of shambles come to stillness.

  That I were not born?
  But you are brother I list!

Brother is not more dangerous than brother
lest pronged, and you have been that
by the great panderers of Olympus,
bethel, theatre to cry harm you yourself had done,
who will soon that to our quick-tempered Zeleian,
then off the oath and shattered truce,
duped like Urias if not able.
Your insult have come. And I will no more
while the war god polishes ornament.
Why not fix this?

  How?

Meet Menelaus.

After the display, further on,
troth berm is barm in this his best lissic,
crouch as curse, burden e'an to his enemy.

I am not but forgive-forged source and will you that.
Otherwise we were like-fathered no more.

  Brother, in every way I attain you
  and I can get three almonds on the head of a banana,
  after the first bite, out of a bowl of almonds, without trying!
  I can get three on the tip, before the bite.
I know I've seen you! But do you not pander me the woman like!   142

And would we were not by these gods postponed!
Cold, like heat, radiates out!

Notes: Troth: I oath, vow! Berm: soil. Barm: decay. Lissic: from lis; – of female; cloth covering for a corpse or to sit on; lissomai – to make entreaty, to plead, beg.

BE A MAN

Multitudes will have passed at the two doors for your being there,
most of Africa and all that South's blackredbrownyellowwhite,
   (Now hail our twins' join of hand across a not gap!)
science end-up in worry would not otherwise say it so,
and the preparation, monumental, will have been mountainous.
But gone now Adam, Abel, the apple, the Garden.
Gone the abandon then charge of Ramses at Kheta;
hands that built lost walls of forever;
logic mis-read of so many as happened;
   Great Past with your suffers in tatters!
Gone the Joans, Brunos, Hopkins' and who knows Vaticansus.
Gone Rousseau, Confessions' comfort in chivalry's lost matter!

Gone Hegel googling Napoleon at Jena, who, The Great Haitian-
'He who opens the way' tortured with treachery `till shatter.
   Gone a Bass Reeves `till we need `em.
Gone Belgium smiling as desecrates Lumumba;
the unknowing heckle of Du Bois `till eyes water,
Quine watching Carnap and his wife manufacture,
Kennedy plying, Malcom, Martin, and Bobby soon after.
And gone 'Much too far out, not waving but drowning,'
someone's humanity and calm `cause they thought they had to.

Aver now and be not aback how who had self-reveals,
vulnerable warrant, as men made much of selves, took much the granted,

who-ought-have-ear, who've been in the matter, who feel and know gather,
ask, Please don't lose him kind Lady on scythe gambit!

`Cause the better do trust the one inside
who is he/she, has a history, and must get along.
And war is the least decisive moment!

Add astern, we say we did, at what men do, have done, anger
our orac into Good Practice, that echo, but only rowdy chaos answers there.
 Now phase transition - make a Just Man! Love old and new –
hate, that took alota space, annihilate! Embarrass yourself,
be called names if must! Say the worlds' civic matters, it might save!
Have-to and do defend as all life does! But be a Human! Be A Man!
who cares for what was given, even as blasts the unsound disbelief
whither aboard some science's biology, chemistry's mix,
or Divine intervene. Don't bop him too much, you'll get through!
 Be A Man save the land, say it's we and Earth!

p.s. or is it ts or ezra, wheatley, rabelais or villon,
maybe walcott, douglass, smith, ellison and fanon?
But friends, whatever It is, It loved you even as you went cold.

Notes: orac for oracular; Phillis Wheatley; "__" Stevie Smith. This poem (since modified)
once attached to a rather be-real, pissed-off, over-worked, dry-scalp, MF-using screed
videoed by the author 02-19-2022, since taken down, that was critic and critique of white,
had the self-rating (the video – Not shown!): "Late Night", "Streaming," so keep your
children and scab-sensitive away!" and is what is referenced as cowardice (the taking
down) in another place, which likens the write for the video.

Among the numbered propositions toward Poetry is the one to do no explication! possibly
accurate, still, in that now I admittedly feel sore and have slapped the boss in the face, but
only gesturingly so! Also: this poem, now Yeats 1919 influenced, may seem brim and overs
at the edges, all high on self and signaling to the bleachers, here I am look at me. But this is
the last thing the artist wishes for his work. Only that it entertain, share and please, even as
aims the efflorescence. And we pray it's more Hi! I see and appreciate you! That thing to
the bleachers. Too, if anyone says there are boundaries in Poetry, aside from good sense
and reason, add responsibility to all that is; press-again on the brevity, you may agree with
me they are probably poetry addressing! JMD!   144

USURPE

Almost acceptable in new suit,
version fed or slightly more on poor precedent
bought thought, its power evident.
Age, creak at bends, was sold on shop floor
for pimply vigor; spritely bounce.
Low cost, in outruns to destroy tethers
pirate business held its course,
Sold! To the man in the blue suit!

Now tau, nineteenth Greek, the nineteenth Greek,
twice lowly pi, took rational 'round the outside;'
- and was jump!
more easily constitute seat for turns'
full circumference to radius,
so old three-dot-one-four, doubled,
floored in the open.

When companies stole and sold intelligence,
bold sprint was pawning cloud chance.
It bared Science, who tried so hard,
had lost its muse, because it had little heart!
Markets, approbitious, induced Reason choose Emotion to usurp;
ghostly secure: Freedom, and Observation: Confidence.
All! To the not news, deal-out the arts, sold!
But many miles and minds behind, or was that ahead?
wakened pupils may tick rascals to track Lady Earth,
her receipts.
Near too broke to feel, before Farmland is bleached,
as Farmers knew the way the world was going,
killing dharma of "whiter hand" tossed out seed from
its toss-out dish, loose the dams baby-retaliations
and that's when Justice, full breach, stood,

manifest from wounded knees shorn.

Notes: Tau (ratio of a circles' circumference to its radius – 6.28) is proposed to usurp (replace) Pi (the ratio of a circles' circumference to its diameter) as the "sacred" number of the circle. Proposed in a 2001 essay by U. of Utah mathematician Bob Palais. Katherine Ann Porter in The Paris Review Interview – The Art of Fiction No.29. "I love the purity of language. I keep cautioning my students and anyone who will listen to me not to use the jargon of trades, not to use scientific language, because they're going to be out of date the day after tomorrow." Approbitious: from approbation (approval). Dharma – Wheel; method.

BLOCKED

A personal view of life there's ample drench; empty
saucepan's ruinous quiet. 'Take it from, these thoughts are
subject being secondary" to turning of hand subsistence bore.

Junctured, roads wedge. Subtle transmissions through amnesia
Movement hid with gravity without hiding.
   Tether, gerund!

Inexperience, aged adolescent develop so raw an edge?
Refuse soft petals of showy rose, foxglove heals,
hyacinth's play, orange blossom's pure that
condemns reluctance's forward chance?
Set-off weight's luck steerage,
'appropriate appliance'!

Serve then motile as quit; dejection: larkspur shown,
tames old purple - the once most monster -
takes from it sense of break and gain quixotic
which:
   leave the creature more than its tail to pursue.

Notes: Rose – love, etc. hyacinth – sport, play. Orange blossom – purity. Purple larkspur – first love.

- 'HERITAGE OF POSSIBILITIES' –

When rampant silver cloud risen rusty effluent fled,
from a likened, distant hunger blindly fed, some twisted back to please.
ἈΛΛᾺ ΣΥ but you pacing opposite, saddened soil trod to cog stance.
To shadow move and blind by the great --- Center: white; First Edge: blue;
Outer: yellow. Looking away, improvised counterbalance,
eyes leave open longer ever those accident, thought, then closed on
inner splot focus; to: open, read red dissipate, new in bare brook with;
caused by squirrel overhead, unseeing in chew, dammin`,
and about to drop what-the-shuck whatever, as rayeous sun was taken in.

That ray's physicality thoroughgoing, 'moment of vision'#,
a retired sept crewed into view at the zero point; and bought,
with sojourn in inner chamber, remnant might
meet lit, dark Neurons at fire, retract, unwire, weather as before;
write nourish which the health flourish is.
  So, as long cultural drainage, and that bit of Hydrogen Parent
that made, and those Hard – seeming no input save base –
gather at the court of image, it may tow and bring home
in 'heritage of possibilities'*, with you, moisture, sibyllic atop –
alive too is rock, here on marvelous Earth!
Being command to imagination, handcuff to you pride!

But a high healed, well'd in the welkin may go, Bolox! That's artsy!
and leave Aerth, in dross and droll, in flashed easy company;
a chase-less identity of pride weal'd entity to co-trive to forward arch,
musin' squash, division choosing: to entertain, as some like... want!
the detriment! Cause some say nothin` pleases Libs like a little suffering!
Then forget Sun, Teraanga, Stone, enlightenment = Daring To Know,

Creativity, Honesty, regional squabbles, tribal tripe, tree inhabits!

It's Critical Thinking fratbotherite!

So, like when -- Maybeyoudon'tsaythe IndigenousWoman'sname

Untilwefindwhowhatistakingthem and Ray Taken Alive, due award,

Lakota Sioux, can anyday bring Sioux Edge to Love of Worth,

which Owns in these not Silent, not non-existent, not freefalling

in filial forests inhab, you will again be akin in mind, gut, brain,

and heart to all Her inhabitants, which is sign of Good Philosophy,

of Fellowship, so – accomplishment, that is a poem! Or,

  like two recent rustle out tree ---- Crow scared-cawing,

  Blue Jay ahide its back, now off with crow's big flap, then peck

  right back at! To check chucklebearing opportunist (like man) rat!

  Like that! ---- 'We may both have to go for our turns,' after Rorty!

  said the ify psychologist; for liberties vary in difficulties;

  and if you don't crib a fit, neither do I!

Hands settle for calm, it being well past bedtime.

  Only incel missiles beak wore-eyes-on; campfire's out;

  some learning outside irrational may yet plot, so we'll finish!

  Aiming to pick in again's ripe season.

  Notes: cog- 'cogitate', cognition. #: From (others) & M. Heidegger's Sein Und Zeit by

  Macquarrie & Robinson: "...Augenblicks." Part I: Div. II; IV, 79, passim. Augen – eye. Blicks –
glances, (blinks). Or "Moment(s) of Vision" - our translators. *: My here - Erbe der
Moglichkeiten from: 'des Erbes von Möglichkeiten' – Div. II; V. 75., ibid. Teraanga – Wolof
word - generosity, warmth, etc. Philosopher Richard Rorty. -Notes are less about showing
what one has read and more about giving credit!

SEARCH FOR MEANING

I

If to center, there is that tunnel Gide,
therefore meditative sanskrita of Elm and Trees of Heaven,
screen between ardent and too teeming road.

This day have saved Frost!
And Stratfordian his Midsummer,
Coleridge's ...At Midnight,
filigreed high place, close-on,
running with treasure to show now angel Mom;
sane themes, in plain fold, the greatest forms.

At top, Sun and Moon go up.
Little group launches paper
feel would tear for a shoulder of stone.
Parents, guard the showmanship of their child.

II

Ringed with surprise, cure of govern,
head level with horizon, that hip of hill watches
what philosopher through drake come walking.
Out to gather plot rust comes with - same doctorate.

Art ate at it, picked about edges of plate, fork to lips:
spout wrought ought just out, 'cept spoil, sidle!

Vlad-like pikes the winter trees are enough stop;
and Revenge the ridiculous, early master un-felt right,
wearies who'd take evangelism for sight.

Deny no idea its easy route;
feldspar ambitions down hill rolling.
Spiked nerve ends oil, eke they too splendid tears out.

149

Five sedans pass rearward windows,

you slip, nemesis smiling, into prayer-clench hands;

antidote riles, hellish martyrdoms singe;

and that wanting a crash-dummy consensus of us

no longer honoured ancestor, dispatches on a careless world, lost.

Poesy strings the vale, light and early morning's shines erupt.

Swells and bothers both come up.

Notes: Stereos [Gk.] solid; see stare. Sanskrita: Sanskrit – refined, perfected. To Andre Gide, French writer, humanist is attributed the statement "Therefore is a word the poet must not know."

STRUGGLE KNOWS

And midday wait not looking nice, wants you lessons without.

The sons of anarchy call carve hell,

catch madness, ill-run education's tide.

Last straw of knowing caught

what teachers shelled for blackening stood out

when vengeance set foot, was raging south;

history at shout, lessons,

eyes on a world shock-eye closed.

In silk, wool, new freedoms' cotton strut,

present with sick-make blanket, shirt,

rhogaleous trouser of hand-down worth,

Contagion's Hymn to Liberty came

sang what would call hate home; make great;

letting-be to shingle justice own

so, a wrong right rose by a blown house door,

and select remembrance Life-blamed the misdeed.
There - 'We say struggle...' with Kwame Ture, for sure.

Who sure in numbers, were counted worse of them
among the punishable, deserving church
garrisoned by cleaves' wicked lash.

Bent end, learned in fearlessness
should have kept, well, protagonists
to bare admission's forgiveness.

Care and a wordhunter were shopping spec!
Controversy, fodder fed walls' solutions tenth
to ignite will-good; valedict to dying tears rent.

Shiner-upright tale'd invalorous.
Yet know, hearts-real shall blare,
in any swept past year, glorious.

The jackal-head by the Fates led
when judgment in baize for less of these,
led backs turned that are sharp turning said,

sweep plain for not-rewards of bad for good;
do not forget Life. How all, each got what, where!
 And in the process further fellows stood;

that meaning in her crystal sockets chime,
redemption in blows and serious crime
'the generosity that comes from justice' could find.

 Notes: Baize: wool napped, pulled to imitate felt. Rhogaleous: [Gk.], ragged, torn, rent, etc. Hrox: [Gk.], cleft (from – torn, rent.) Valedict: Valedictory – parting, farewell. "the generosity..." G. Du Maurier, *Trilby*.

Out, Wild Running

Spill, buzz, hiss, doer of good - Heart, out wild running;
meanness under cap, and break are back in from oarship.

Campus unheight where addlepated, sure-thing advocate
raced obscure at work-poets are not mocked, but
the old grass on verdant couch is out of its hole wild running.

Right-self gavel on brigand day, scramble will on lighter fare.

Years describe eyes-out-at-night when she left or him.
When the twelfth eldest tree was decimated.
Forced, wild running.

It means so much and costs so little to stand not gelatinous with hurt,
when heads' not up the splash, but sound in a drive to Liberty
over they would take out, wild running.

Water, food for all, banner poverty expurgate awhile
milieu among millennia know nothing that deft effect,
only ill grates the hay men make, out wild running.

THE Landscape!

There had been something in it, certain times betrothen.
It has, since tacit compel, make a toy with, these range ravings
I do ankh, but in the fly-off scream and angers' unjust scrape clear the clear.

Much of baren. Without live moisture cold-coupled from cloud
like in the old days wordery too was saves and culprit,
and seemed to clasp chief cruel from same amusement.

Time to toddle on and some place to come toddle from secure;
claim cup, limp, slide and sidle timed rife in garnish. Anything
but that done to self with a knowing.

We had silverbacks there that day, and large whale' sonar lent.
   Days later sometimes when it was goofball hot,
   a child with a bat would appear and the believing lights beat out of.
   But those were mostly holy days, holy for bat bearers.
I told Fred the angels had come. Fred said no just some devil dressed like `em.

And kept me my own council then; never again strife
to arrange cools from a thistle bum sty.
That orb that sat sure it was easy for passers to accomplish
since Original Cause was/is hiding and keeps an eye on
was sight straight in the hierarchy. No misread this feed.
 Having had, spun, spied.

TRAGEDY TO AID RESCUE OR THE BOOK OF OrAnd

Hear in a south stairwell, frenzy of feet, controlled stampede
and sweat heat of bodies-close, with power off – that was ride, lark,
wild swing jump `round landings with all well, Tragedy
the goat song saying, slowed now to hold as it nevertheless read
notch with precipice; who, always, perceives concerned,
clear of Escapes' intent, delaying hurrah! and eureka!
 spoke whisper to Aid, also turned captive the welter.

Out, in a Book of OrAnd, with the eagles, note floats air. Is scratch
double-sided - abstract at envelopes' crease. Scents of cinnamon, pine needs
and a lot of wet turf with open-air not factory, jet, fire, or risen topsoil pierced
tray the hope, break into nose, I might run! have mind magick swirl.
Spring's young tree pups goal their place Tri Holy Sun!
Music tickles the fare; I careen my scratch and stare.
A few Giraffe crane top crop. Lion, still the child knew, essences how and ear,
to chase and check a fleet-foot through. Room still for crocodile, alligator,
all long-time cousin cavern aimed and for the keep of virtue
that on those walls was written; heaved lift to life that later
 from stone to wood to keyboard feature.

Securely, honed reap-and-roll got the red blood boil, but
cup out of hands, Keystroke in the central computing system - ça va? –
blew one Josephson Junction, `sweet violence!' to reach his dumb ass,
 and leave as left insensate to mis-calculate!
Opening texts to no potential difference, ahoyed! that Konigsberg sage,
not hamper, not expelled like Fichte by Schiller and Goethe,
`Concepts are an achievement,  not a gift!'  `Duty! Not happiness!'
`Duty which leads to happiness!' showing the way to a slice
 `The thing in itself'# did the labouring man issue!

Aid, pulling its too-short shirt said - With potentiality for being,
like The Galileo Galilei – all kinds of Lion on there! We roved there might be   154

accept of low sum, as young job applicant, High-fives timein where.

But the young barely line for that now!

Without doubt the great responsibility, in the red of morn, was Everyman's

(they agreed) in and on resultant Anthropo -cene, - in potentia –

allegory to growl, a few orders of tragedy to transport and hap

toward the highest realities; those sometime tedious that do affect an age;

  comedies bibing, a past yet slips the stage!

In discovery I cheered Milton; and thanked the Music of the Spheres

as with a distressed Galileo wizened; as Galilean, the old hand pled,

"This, God likes it!   So, I must like it!"   As Soul, that Hundred Percent,

of one of the most aidfull of his Age – in redirect of the listening,

upright Universe, splendidly eyed plinthed formerly estranged,

now doubling conscious streams that on their Always comfortable perch –

anxious extremes, known for no room for insertion – true bowed,

  touch-typed, and maintained how!? the whole-iest urges now!

Notes: `sweet violence = tragedy'. # - Immanuel Kant via Bryan Magee, Melvin Braggs' In Our Time or from The Durants (Will, Ariel) Thx Rocky C! The whole-iest urges = for instance, [out of a long list of expressives] John Searle's "Unified Conscious Field" (and of course Kant's "Ding an sich, thing-in-itself" is problematic, but not in conception, in stretch/add of perception; knowing you can't see the observed from all perspectives, vector points. Yet another useless controversy. And it was always there, this field, ether, environment, in what may be called, with accuracy, our belief-knowing inherent, Intuition, what Indra had to do with, or not! The whole Without with its first element, Hydrogen for match. Which is as good an understanding as Dark matter and energy (dark to us) scenarios for Universes' supposed missing matter or bang. Ideas sift through the field, to, at, and atmospheres' no barrier. And then, with extreme inaccuracy, someone from 'race', state, financial or other partisanship supposition(s) says give up on Globalism, when we Are All fish in this bowl, and removing the Air will (K)ill All, whom our Chomskys and laugh-filled Ellsbergs, ala Democritus, should grant ear to. Or not!

VOTER

They want you beloved, to their errors betrothed -
Ian Masters' bilious billionaires!   E' tu que?
  Say then, with brilliance born, conceive you a wrinkle,
in favor, that suspects contaminant and so,
slide off animals' rendered backs again,
  cause your arrival had to be that!?

And say, among sons, daughters, wives and possessions
accept you your ongoing evil away-from;
and with the grieving everywhere pray a vater unser or Our Father;
read something of Shakespeares' bush-burst busts of labour
or of the port-wine poetry of Neruda to said children.   Or,
  the sweet team of too much bravado.   Do that!

Then, ripe Tuesdays and round Mondays collate
your balance-finding atoms; Wednesdays and everything after
keep an easy-breath light lit, that against thrown, any slight,
you intreat, do not hamper!

End memet; brief Gloria sing and signing No Complaint! document,
whence you reach by no accident, but desert,
via participations' manifests,
the holy, precious, sane, public vote accomplish!

  Note: memetic.

IN PRAISE OF PLAIN MEN

The sound would be glare spectacular.
Someone later said 'bring children, fools, dim-wits...
they all that seem to instinctively get what it is...'
thinking of a thing evident, like war is no good.
And the fast mist is hot summer air's comfort.
Tots unconcerned, are still new to anger;
their olders, adolescents are rehearsing anger to be
adults of all years listening in their chairs.
And with this great pay Praiseworthy I'd assent you.
You've been so kind to the heart.
"Ubi bene, ibi patri" our motto too
our country too should we land it;
Plain presenting our beck, and tall
and Love our call out of the whole wild running,
said square-bracket day has worth noble disciplines.
Emile and Sophie are sturdy and are happy,
a good map of clearances spreads in heads.
The old work, old, seams new down back of change,
there 'the vulgar in their own language have been spoken to'.
And that 'white house with green shutters'
and fine tiled roof lone on its hill, yours!

Notes: "ubi bene, ibi patri." – "where one is (I am) well/good, there (is) (my) fatherland/country/home; Quoted by Jean-Jacques Rousseau, Emile [1224], p. 256.

OCTAVIAN AT THE STATUE

Battles, fates, destinies; pride, power, Republic.
Civic wills only brash slacker Two-extremes-over-abrades knows.
- Fort Randall, Kennebec, Murdo the Badlands.

There lies bait near Milan in then faun Alps, methink,
plausibly somewhat near a "Y" shaped lake on its head,
morning mists clothed in, the story of how between the pine above
and chestnut below, Queen's Road on and perhaps about, an emperor
comes upon the Ka thing of a Brutus in that age, his family enemy.
Probably, Liberator Lucius, our chronicler says, as he our August
angers the stony view, of his favored, paged noble Roman enemy.
In summoning thereafter every magistrate of the place, claims he smilingly -
somewhat for reaction & sport - themselves: as not friend!
Aye, traitor! for harbouring this, if statuesque, uncle/father killer,
enemy to he, divi filius, of his lord. He, nephew and robust son
whose voice '`fore Jupiter, Horace also, poet freedman-born, raised.'

Our philosopher then, this Dryden done, whom Clough-described – Dryden:
"hasty, well written, inaccurate but agreeable to read...")
(a-buck) multi-amanuensis) - affirms him saying – 'it was his once enemy
stands there! though debugged, debraided. The likeness of hands;
mystery-like that drawn across centuries, can draw, gravel for blood,'
hairs on end; disinter mind for ancestor, heir, and deposit on stout Time,
up-short taken re-looks, falls-memory's retuned rhyme; grand in outwash
of lithic sadness, hinter crime,
    that on the loop wind, pushes and possesses all.

Well, in great fear his hidden jest, they scrape noxious to `deny being enemy.'
Until that early August, points the statue, smiles. And 'Commendation Gauls!
for staying friends in adversity. The statue shall Remain!' edicts out.
That became the triply tribute to these Citizens!   Evertheless,
suffering under thumb for even more evenings, torture was! The slide of Rome!   158

Notes: Lucius Brutus, Liberator of Romans: Plutarch, "Pop(Pup)licola" p.118, 123. Marcus Junius Brutus. 'Ka: (the selfsame) In Ancient Egypt thought to inhabit the statues of kings and deities; the double of, one's soul, as if.' Our Philosopher – Plutarch. 01 January 42 BC, nearly two years after the assassination of Julius Caesar on 15 March 44, but before the final victory of the 2nd Triumvirate over the conspirators who had taken his life. Roman Senate recognized him a divinity. Horace: Ode I.1. He was therefore referred to as Divus Iulius (the divine Julius), and his adopted son styled himself Divi filius (son of the deified one, son of the god). The fuller form, "divi Iuli filius" (son of the divine Julius) was also used.

Multae sunt mansiones
in domo patris mei

These flows I look and love on

are brown, green and rise;

ecstasy waves in solid flood

balance for mind. Like man must

come to think of himself, with Earth, his charge,

in the water of space time.

This will I think add the experiential fluidity found,

generally, mathematically needed; 'Be like water my friend!'

very movement of the medium itself, but I could be wrong.

A soul, its palpitations, glory do the escape

but wash over and Life what He has hand-made:

a homing provençal high roof for the eyes,

with the good land papa'd, and bestowed every thought,

action clear for quiet wait His announcement.

   Beam great eyelet!

Notes: John: 14, 2 – "Many are the apartments/rooms/mansions in the house of my Father." or "In my Father's house are many mansions." "Be like water..." Mssr. Bruce Lee. Provençal: adjective and noun. (fem.-ale, pl.-aux) Provençal; Provence – roughly Southern France.

THE RIGHT OF SPRING

Stalls fence-less lavish open,
scramble and never check pour caught
unrepent freedom's net.
On subject, Fresh beguiles Hold
with shows humane service lease
to exposition and declarative sentenced
to invisible, noble laurel collect,
in a soon-filled silence never regret
like 'liquored Rabelais',' beetle-browed Voltaires,
skipping Gides with their kef in North Africa.
All alike other hijacks, whose "transports" and convenience cup,
since sober is not saint nor sized to actual's delight;
  skip me over my onepuff©!

Come money-back guarantee sartor;
you need only the mirror. And not solely
those handling letting-dame's waist
keep free self-murder on convention's raised deck,
which comes ala' concealment, a behest
to drink, torrent its clearer and consume
just the intellect of benison;
or pry-thy prats from ply-they schools,
to diamond Inspiration inferior, twice.

So Men play at and intend radiant.
Soon, months sore the bit are all green in mendicant.
And terrible tendence to torture selves,
leaves for dark unrest like honest at its start.
Men free seer acrimon swing to, if consequent,
meet on the great green bench, of her cool-born continents.

Notes: [Bonheur: happiness, felicity]. Letter XXII: On Mr. Pope and Some Other Famous Poets – Francois-Marie Arouet – Voltaire. Beetle-browed: overhanging, jutting, suggestive of a squint (disapproving). Bumf: toilet paper: [Brit]: paperwork.

THE FOLLOWING LOVE POEMS

A man throws so much the little, clock's centuries fare;
akin idris, provident, whether Brahman or no, everywhere
tangling in languages; scant meld knolls; distant Tenor breaks through;
teary trounce evacuates tremble; he self-calls self proper fan!

Oh! Mass suffrage for the men, they'd have that
as rap on edge of pinnacle Sibyl; that house renews poorer!

Haps we go about explaining much; prices slash; splashes
our Simonides of crosses, keep the bees in that; insurance cedes height.

Un corazón, where tamp clam-happy poems, the slow getting-have
and chance-out? Are what pages, canvas, own footnote?

PREFACE TO (PATHS IN AIR)

If appulse in hike or climb what would outdo,
clamour over that ledge if have to!
No eating tabernaculars; but praying's there!
Ten'll take twenty if I'm wrong and
we'll meet on the other side of the cue!
This, Paths In Air, is what I seem to want to consider
in front of the last few published in recent work! JMD!
   Placed first in a pile after kind of losing it, here we are, and
given under lesser heading does not lessen, as once it was; a thread
easier to travel, I said to self.   Yet, another but – that of what's up with us?
Human beings Homo sapiens sapiens? What gleans from this moniker;
We this With the Other lives that matter, which, griffin, be all?

   As Prior then, as first principle, how to achieve;
how data digital and material muster,
and the best for all to be in solidare cause?
 Excused! Your stray eye just there as finished. And out goes the wish
All the best in all seasons, and health years round or oblong to you!
 Lastly, akin those refuges who shipped selves, clung eleven days to a rudder;
only to have Spain again not want, drags this from:
I've seen screen heroes, but man Africa, immigrants worldwide! Real Life Ones!
Determination, like tortoise in his living - to move to rest to move to rest
to do torque tango with time, with God's help please! against the odds –
because you have to Take Care of All Life it is hoped, is the best achieved
 of achievable!

PATHS IN AIR

Paragon of life   There for the taking.   And what is air?   What
times-great, friendly bond of gases we breathe?   Better ask, fast!
    So, here's this guy, all attachments guying while pull, gather, reel;
throws silk and balances like a G.O.A.T. or giant, and it occurs
    ... heck! I can't do that!   Sure, I could try to impress spider
    in the zero-barrier zones, her own boss, like me mine,
    where meld and melding of Indra's weave holds blare quanta
    and each in sensethought is first and last, but there, and can talk.
But here, engage the straightahead Father Joseph!
    Trust musement; move to null as 'impossible',
    `cause what the heck, too little will be found there,
    and some questions by man may be answered, but...

Here's this guy doing spin, plait of paths in air,
sleek-wire hold on four directions the once, even in wind...
 then I get there's upset with my watch – he's shirtless for sun,
got cowboy hat on, (   ), amuses terribly - and watches me -
Then yep! I guess s/he's cut the paths going in sort of one direction,
toward phone lines and tree further out while those opposite
lets pull with swing and pissed hop, to the hot tin roof
But I was thinking, Oops, not! Then yep! soon enough, hop! Yep Hot!
    `Cause I've been surprised on that roof before!

NOW BOUNTY

History! Mother has filled tub and turned on her shower.
In-total, drenches clean and easy as a storm sidles overhead.

What dooms awake in imagination
when approaches vocal Storm, that boom dang!
that in afflatus, what she has left behind
was, is, seems such a gift and could be nothing otherwise?

In the story and philosophy of men they think they have truths
someone said, but what they have are possibilities at hatch;

when against life's strains and many disparagement,
at every point, one has for Good, laid one's own 'I was!' down,
not much but gratitude can attach,
for oneself and the whole in the dust, as he, she goes along.

Both hands holding, devising in detention as M. Delacroix
(before Heidegger (in trans.) piloting almost the same language) did
and let loose: that 'What the wisdom of the ancients discovered
before making so many experiments
must necessarily be accepted by us, and we must submit to it.'

Note: Delacroix's Journal – Monday, 23 April 1849. See M. Heidegger's Sein und Zeit;
Macquarrie & Robinson trans. P. 40

ON PASSING OF THE ST. LUCIAN

Of Life and Love!
Of Master workers!
  All things go to rest!
  Sure the breath is Life,
  it's bond Love!
His contretemps, his peripeteia with
the decidedly tricky, non-poetic
pis aller against the celebrated
that good literature in its adopts of market behaviors
tried on him toward the end
will, like in earth's change of seasons,
sputter, fall and dehisce with the worst of `em,
till the flora he sparked in full write and paint,
that has never done anything but – bloom does,
for discoverers again and again.
  The Maker is thanked for you Sir,
  now further above!

TRITE

Oh how meet fine would sit table,
lark entertain, shave time.
The way offense toiled clapcheap shots.
The way sustain's final give-up south dropped
off pop march on crazy, un-principled behavior.

How, oh how green, molder of task,
shoulders schiller its good-crop mask,
that down cathedral Time, spurts swart,
marks inside-out to find,
there in that thinking it possible
to be better at love than previous was,
something of truculence seize such
as would blink the eye and mind a very god!

But for nervous tyrants, the less popular kind,
nothing was possible that wasn't crime.
And it's not what men don't know that banks them fall,
but realities forgot, again and again. That's all!

Note: schiller: a kind of brown, (copper) color usu. of some stone or mineral (ish).

DIGITAL ACCESS CROSS CONNECT®

A pine needle mid-air on its thread,
as one tree nods: she's company!
and tagged tug of terry cloths are past would dun.

Had you pasted here drum hands,
seen men do this without glasses a few times,
you'd be much at topic Quebecois!

So drag drail or dram the shuts if trail thick dust.
Hoe-hup breaths terrif if dangers are not handy-in-from-window
or such as are obeying, from what ails, officiancy does.

Dross double doss, oops!
The tenant sees all that is not tryst's confinement!?
To the right, to the left our scups then?

Tonnage and mile, meter over dolphin.
Shadow, the first photographer,
to Death and Sleep, sends convince-of-worth.

The dare midden ends - ten to ten Men have Good In Them!
    But that shirt has a few hours on it!

And there, exact un-shakable,
pieces mean something when Life were out of tune.
Or rang the Seven Freedoms Frostian,
active romps sent to detain grip assailant,
with the yellow sea-snake guardian too.

    Nan has you and me dacs if we're ready!?
    (Stand) At the hash tag please!

Notes: ® DACS: AT&T, Lucent Tech. product, then. Dun: plague, pester; marked by dullness and drabness; gray-brown color as of a horse. Drail: drag and rail. Dram: a small portion, etc. Hoe-hup breaths: from Documentary movie about an Australian drummer that goes to Korea to visit "Intangible Asset No. 82" Korean native drum master. Midden: Dunghill, refuse heap, etc.

RESIGNATION (Once called Plod)

On oaf fears! as she touch-taps the walk and you boggled, watch.
How slow can Tarantula? So, size is not a croc!?

Led, bare-foot, without shoe, sock, to nourish nightmare,
of scissored mandible sunk in where she, a specie of Gargantua....
is by something bigger shadowed... Wilbur's Owl?

But nature, by battery-light, as this sort of spider, does not
in its scurry even hurry. Resignation to moment finds
   both there and more and more, here.

Proverb

Not to add to or take from; will go fear in hand God!

 'These things are too wonderful' Great King!

A companionable heart;

the form of a woman ungarnished.

Sweat of night on blade and leaf; all the waters are.

A tree, any tree sentry enwound.

Every place meadow, valley, dell allowant.

Each rise, holy of land still called hill, canyon, mountain.

Rock and boulders' - stone cousin, mascot of intuitonal slowing;

physical layout of home.

Her picture going stroke the cosmos. Milky Way zone.

The way conspicuous species, in litotes, cast a kind word,

or lithotrachilos finally awe, and eager, grope sad gratitude,

words of wisdom, and again heirloom animal kingdom,

 insist human is but one part maximillius!!!!

 Now, Alleluia!

Notes: Proverbs; 30, 18 – Solomon: "Three things are too wonderful for me," Litotes: understatement in which an affirmative is expressed in the negative of the contrary. "I'm not unhappy!" "He's not a bad player!" Λίθοτράχηλος: lithotrachilos – stony; stiff-necked – Julius Caesar.

THE WHISTLER - FROM THE INSIDE

A deep wood shadowy path we, if you with me.
Nine ways pierce threaded wall.
Inhabitants whistle, grump, root, follow smells,
light steps with our Emmanuel - Reason our Beatitudes,
Understanding stomp. Peer we open hands, Muses there!
Two, matter oblique at electron level, transpare, immute, run –
that way, we think, Life does in growingout's hand.

'Yet, wide the lands of see, writ in Flood; as some constitution
join, band, group, mend abrupt to some owing need
as worm miss-far-the-measure burrows, and away cedes,
- we would save Fly Earth about Her holy axis!

'Shallow astray sought laugh; days of joy, adumbrate,
blink dumb!' (around a deadfall we skip, saving fun!).
' Mind and Heart to fairly treat the fool in, he of measure,
with other minds and hearts dissect universes of 'markless words.'
Down, lothario, ill-lodge-o, traitor on wall poised to fall, crack;
quench one thirst at ebb and expense of another! Or
the bell perched, was it rung?

'I myself, add uber, clasp craft-and-align-with choice in pleasing,
grateful, yesteryears' joinless cabins that bent to
in prayer of simple bard!

Gracious Land grate, carrying another side of the sing that was song
across, so no crush and curse because of, the ships core this reactor is,
might blast chance of necessity in conflate, of which we've seen some!

'Nod and dock the simple in difficult - Butterfly, professing complaint
society's snags, you may drag, smash, duck, weave full-stop and feint,
as arts' a way, rude to display - sate, not-safe sail, that surely comes

when holes we've dug, are best evidence of. And because of this
 I would not be a man! You overstand!

'There we Cain, look anywhere the thing cannot...
Add little faith in off-puts to chastise for not showing up invest,
as always.   Bolt oh Reverse, stay! Obvious late, lilt tilt
She chambered defines; born to loose, burn, disaster fall,
from goings in or comings out - go ahead and toll
the blasts and canker dear before more Breaths trail off -
control satellites in medium scell that his or her flag
in high atmospheres paint... Oh my atmospheres! Hold me
that they not traditional Day's Blue cream off, allowing destroyers'
future work in upset: all horrors having preened long then!'

 I hear you Woodpecker; Jam on! White Nearly hads that one!
 Sod, you good man --- seen, met in familiars – where unfortunate end,
 Comfort smile, tedium welcome and three and four allow yield
 the numbnuts set to subtle half-was, half-wasn't advance in strolls;
  mark old clamps on cities kept, while rural siphons sums -
 those now ground aches from, so water evaporate, holes to pull succumb;
 and hot winds the fragile window careen, punch, bumpy hum.
Effort, even capitalized and back-from-abyss, Come! Do not back up!
 Say, preach, be a something can come out for, Love,
 as highest way through learning From The Inside you!

OUT ON THE EDGE OF THINGS

Box elder, Rhododendron, Delphinium;
come chiral blat, splat with two-fisted Arkidelphian,
chip nail being the worst in the Master's understanding gift,
as Thumb misses to be let in. Praying others are second kin,
finishes he close to scumb, nails and knuckles mind;
Peace to secure, crowd tine.

Just on the rim, alternate, draw open,
limn pen's introduced pages.
For you have in suckle worth dreamt,
who deems now fitness of five, who calls dexterous
to work in hive of kilters' contraire-grasp.
Nightmare's chaff will not! Catching apples at a back door fast.
There is little know not what to do with.
Keeping balance, the purest.

   Note: Scumb: short for scumble.

THE PROFANE MARSH RABBITS

Lay the foxtails, dandelion, sky and close earth enclosure.
Have, Don't listen to them! the Why? of no good answer,
 Their feet are wet, we have no precedent!
The with, They do not the dry lands inhabit! that group story
to fall - no peace. But keeping durance, some of us...
 Come on, they're still much the same as we, let's listen.

 Stunned, eye tides and seas of gnat and pollen
soon to be fly and flower early the spring of a wet winter.
Catch califluent rush of water rustle side of a road down which
whole colony of bees went aiming swift as headturn and hearing;
 made belief of for-soul fearing before, off, summer flew.

 Sync with, "Man, that cullion! 'shit and religion always
 stinking in concord,' to quote one old arbiter, leaves him
 forever eating slice in a harrow, may deserve dreg employ.

"Too-big or small for justice column bony undrape. Or
like such Enochs, Elijah, another few; things a cloud or wind might –
Possibility at ride – painting, forming, or panting forming? –
under 'Preexistent' all things realize themselves –
make joint with The Great I Am as is we're told. And hearing
assists each to each, the come together of rabbits and men,
to debt guest respects, may yet for Cease sue – their current
 most worthy; with no more digs, no mining welcome!"
 A clap ! But grope 'southward' another ten desert rabbits,
unseen, lardered fay now sway lemon grass, tossing diedains!
 There, a third right not left larger cleft, another against
(why is this invisible), like (that's similic) in others' current precincts
unveil curious trust-crime commit of part-analyze - with,
'There are many views!' And 'both-sides' shortcuts still; stopped:
the-best-for-all to be wild, broken for own on and brought about.   173

Foolish-slaughter, effective stealth, ptoliportho that breath-air stole
en route was part the clean miss accrete of 120 times 3 in torus
at axis; or 6, or 9? that has, yes 12! weep service-tears in the dejoint –
Opposing hum 'Ohs!' We, 'with opposite frequency 'uncoup…'';
assenting good advice of one, and trust we sleuth study when we sees it.

So, a tusk, a roar; a blast adore; cowed-yoke wouldnot to-life be broken
fored Reasons' stops that gout. And quick brave trying un-yoke with
utterly irresponsible Chance; good-of-whole at lookout charged, anew –
they could not without doubt say what was affecting the marsh rabbits,
wouldn't do same to they themselves, you others, us. That in above of
clear truths' oathed, they could not say there was no fuller kernel;
no wider birth; only opposites opposing along a chain of inseparables;
and neither 'No more grasses entire!' as good queen Sense, in her trees would;
nor grand incautious stir of black to white, white to black that
circle in their circle as reason should, have restrained their bite!
Instead of Dread! Sure'd in giant footfalls coming in the great teaching
moment that, "Happiness retain! Join! And save your dumbasses!"
 was louding from somewhere distinctly they heard.

Notes: 'shi# and religion…'; 'southward'- Ezra Pound, Canto LVI. Ptoliportho -"city-
destroyer/sacker"- Epithet used by Homer of Achilles, (others) and other Greeks in 'his'
Iliad. Cf. Bk 24 - Zeus in his kind-going anger.

OVERVIEW

A mesh! mind, catches thankful - fallings, kind of wraps,
 so fits uncomfortably, too tight often!
  Had opportunes better in paying attention to that,
and BRICsobrian, like the priest argued father and mother forward
  exuberant! from intolerance! and the fluid center of a florid Earth.

African-taught early Europe with Hegelian dialectic - Robert Browning/
Wheatley/Emersonian/Wordsworthian humanism have to see survive -
A Mr. President _____ to a President _____ to... synthesis!? Yes!
  And astonishment!! May barely escape a bag of sins in that!

Often, heads aright, notice the long, slump ships of eve
come on what swift wants. And grump, dry backs of far hills
desert winds scratch.
      California Grays' squirrellin'-up the area with newborn.
      - One, splot branch near nest bottom - oh missal minutes!
  seems very much with sir sunset in trance.
      - Corvidae teach their young crow etiquette, that dance.
   - Jay on roof, too, considers curious view east,
curvature like that on The Divide at this height.
- And push-up lizards in close-formation swallow diet pester-flies.

- Many another and alert-kind of many more Will here, but some,
with one pine-elder jacked - bad watering - like old bear come
to bad sleepy cover for nightly naps; stopover vultures,
their anchor tree gone, screen the horror in go-by
and will probably not come back.

Better arrangement! Couple some valence. Here align the power
of the beating pump; as Nature leads some astronauts shyly to,
going through what some call le Overview spiritual experience,
that fits and littles - that we, average citizens,   175

with eyes better held on true Earth-home might also realize.

And from determined orbit, soft, our select jewelry sky hung;

the bull, the bear, hunter, washer, dryer, station with the seat;

branded products, services and programs - Oh mind! Bend backs

so we sort of live, alive! That so-called hegemon, archon,

may we beware to become.

There, lead to raised responsible, welcomed hair-shirt of Saint Francis,

that empties I's and suits whys to beam and learn,

as over-horizons dim go, for proper prostrations.

Note: BrazilRussiaIndiaChina countries. Valence: power, capacity, wield.

ISEMATICS - THE MATHEMATICS OF ABUSE

4 x the window + 6 x the door = the imperfect score
of prop and prime ÷ the jet fuel that held hostage,
that polled high as disturbance. It was given
life – time = death; life = time and time life,
but they only knew the sprout as call to breath
rallying in, out, away; there were turnarounds. Ends?
Rarely did they know of those. But they agreed
Is = AreBe^2© + The overall anxietal-aspect
of consciousness ~ ± ½ the relative reality©.

One said, Like Pushkin, 'she booked him a conquest,
but he had some self-service there too, no doubt'!
They asked = if most of learning ends cynical, of what use?
Is there room in Poetry for the mishmash + new worlds +
'hamburger's song' + defending Democracy + the compact =
the sacred, as She rests beside accomplishment never?

To be denied is the Ritz of good work; alone-capture has no equal +
the qualification of means lies dormant as all eat from endangerment;
and each creature itself creates with Maker + environment is said.
 Ergo, enough rarely satisfies + all wanted = achieved with fight
with Without; where what-use-any-of-it + doom to all appears ≤
one's own importance, where sums do not sum, and more needs added,
 like water, that increase, considered in Its fullness.

IMAGINARY HAVEN

...Arrival! through margins finally stop, bump against this bumpy way,
haul breath! Being near, the signboard there we read, detached...
"|__"Songline", Saluté! Complimenti Carnyx! A-horn! - Traveler, you have
run the track and spare brigand. Enter this Brundisium, where when sun hide
and sea, flat, lap dark, taking breaks behaving, war wheels rut no stone. Proud
 at the end of trails, `sa 'real raggamuffin', a God-protect of the vault Will
and not a one of phalanx and strict overwhelm raised tower, vied feat build.
        Admonition had no holiday! Still was work!
      Latitude measured Caesar, Goad-To-Good Pope, our chance!
      and scoundrel along these ways - Virgil, hale and shoulder strong,
      not lost to fever; Horace more than clocked ami & amie; questioned
      better road, recount he, smart, clapped smile exchange of labor.
      And Milton, Pound, we found not unavailable; only saint surpliced
            these altar.   Hail Father Hefler of the Hand!

      Condor big'in passin' overhead did sooth! We had an Eden then,
      more Heaven than that, and had it who heaved more than thought could,
       in notice, in place, averred & intact, for learnings approval apt!
Wizardry, cuffed docket, had to tight as favorably ceded Intuition,
that corker! dealt 'seen' the disarray, drunkard; end sightless dissipate
      cloying cozily, coping swamp Along refuse avenues with Unrest, if that!
         oh! the rent! tempt to quizzy treacheries to quit close of good on!

      "And poet, this is 'your element!' Learned in the histories, pried
      Philosophy and Literatures, never but to art subject, we said - forth!
       Dump profit, enter virtues' bout, greased-palm lucre no more!
       But hold! One needs space to write however put in basket.
            Space is time and place there're the taxes!

      'Pentaur, Aesop, Homer and Hesiod having the gavel, kept it!
Plato gearing to forms, told of his Africa ('Egypt or Libya'); and again, again
      admitted union and with the poets and philos (natural or not)   178

one after another, after another, in same pews sat. Sensei and Sadhu
had Amos, Jesus, Socrates, Thespesion, Mencius, among more, kindly,
trying for handle, scrutinize. Aristotle, spoke on all, but some, " farther Sir!"
And subject rabble's vulgus dolt, cast he render high share for place common.
Teaming, break-aparts gathered. Asunder, no disaster did court.
Equality, and Fraternity, and You, Fine Justice, superior argument, prevailed.
None were excused for crimes against the innocent!

"Unsuspecting, overd't no rail by coward cozen,
None attacked a physical inferior to their extension and said victims assail
did Life Lesson - threaten no life, food as proviso! And Flowers naming selves,
congressed-new with ready pollinators and deep-sea boat attackers
repairing man's insanities well.

"Plastics, only of the George W. Carver plant kind, went, unclogged land
and sea. Age-old combustion stopped, 'seeing' what had done, and sat
no more skies; thoughtless hearths, stack, and ill-will's car smoking
awares' haven! Gossip, crass continually, bit lip, refrained! Media had
no more the license he-ha! tossing salads and lives. We loved that "Maecenism"
was same as 'stimulate the arts', Aurea Mediocratas as G&R; and with All!
The golden apple ply we shared, saying Fare it each as the fair and thankful way!
Ordering here, fateful days in passing patient Heaven, and so be it?__|"
Mouths awry after shake of dissonance above blink eyes; rattled Brain!...
We sat in that novel silence, squint that sign, better part of a trying noon
deciding that was why there was no one there, only webs patrol the region.

Notes: Maecen... E. Pound's Letter(228) D.D. Paige. "Aurea", Horace.

TO THE LANDS OF FAIRNESS. AMONG THE GRAYBEARDS

Pentheraphobe as fought. She won.
Quest for Egyptian grawlix in so small then, at confess,
to plain old Phoenician, Assyrian; hoped backing to a somewhen
moderns might to Greece from handy Dark Continent,
as did fair ancients, as does archaeology,
the prior credit for the hand-off leave.

Well, this detains and causes, if brief, mention,
speaks directly and ships to The Lands of Fairness À la Buisson,
to not forget what some, though their near books and best interests will
verify 'what they gained,' quoth Watts, 'on the round-about,
they lost on the swings,' have forgotten in un-fairfull pattern
in the Unified Field; that quotable jungle-jims scaling would.

Being from this estranged, the fence and T-boned corrals skip
along with cries out of stiff containers that now sea how dull
ownership keeps its nasty, schatty seat; and would Not! Fair teach!

Among the greybeards, honestly betrayed,
mortal gravity's heave-y arm rally waves sag;
drapes palp-fear about feasts at corners of mouth
and urges Age's unsweet sounds aloud with Sophia's (Loren)
'keep it to yourself' crack – to creak and meet less at good finish,
    for aging well's coincidence.

Now, with Ayea Ashay Ayea! Philodendros imitate,
and sail in any-yacht there; mid-day being delicious!
Fortnights' less-woody horror down staggers the mind
and harbour peers passage.

Lured telleries, with neither way nor means, murid leave sighted,
course plot and are aboard! Where, likely, some young, sent to overcome,

cover ummm significant insignificance, never really him, her or it, of old,
again: the job, the voyage: became the one that left and never came back,
infected by Young's Spectacularity now have little distinct memory of.

在greybeards间, women? Bless this! But how is soft so soft and live?
Stubborn toward twos' entwine move; and how is gain so achieved, so narrow?
Yet, the work, there is, to toughen, expand,
teach a universe how it's done. Prayers and possible judicious.

الآن بين greybeards, laugh! Unburdened, naked branch, are favoring life and
by time in grade, under overworked-ease, vorfreude large sighs breathe.
 Evil never advances every way; institutional pound slows,
and constraining filters' blind details' oblivious shucks momently-in's,
cynic defense wrongly abled have too long put up with.

To life and a universe un-grown into conceptions well? Your gifts divine.
Such knocks of no-knocks' appreciations for no-knocks favored,
having lost full-dimensions' wisdoms – armoured at stack -
is trailed in un-track of savior Night to whom gored aid unfurls.

в настоящее время среди Седобородых, they hate us: whites!
A friend said and would To The lands Of Fairness and out of their
every twenty years' dead-going praxis deep hole of hate come!
But now among the graybeards, more ambitious, strongly bid,
recall, manly Christ! Manly among detractors, manly fore, manly did.

So, among your greybeards, perhaps there are two stories of tree out there
that are buoyant! whose sinkwater unwaste outer fingers' stretch;
grateful the balance in drought those arms. Yours, the clear ichor carry,
till un-thinking, fouled with un-friendly ingredients down septic
that did plenty bash, Sorry!!!

Tears. But now then – what you've done good - a jug, kelly'd and passed
in a satellites' bright. And this into books: Agenor! Bold! Poet Judicious,

milled midst causative vates' onslaughts, self-referential differential
in calculus let that construction serve!
  And even if a Marley in a mirror, Valour, loose the unknown,
let natural predator to hopes infestatious churn; as through your doing,
done, no more worries! ballast, staff unknown; and let no more homopredations
playdate watch!

Inter haec murorum senes (among these greybeards), as you will, remember
whip appendage to non-whip hand, that one long post posits
rough-typed and up by sheer strident struts strew for glacial stars' tack
to steer by right round a subdued expanse of light.

And without delay among those graybeards (parmi les barbons)
chase chooses two steps couldn't so four practice where effort's inch.
There, Evening's career is built upon a seat,
while energized feetly, in sore societies, found pedestrian,
as rough roads creased with irresponsible Media's fictions,
gap complete fabric, so machined therewith into force festive
and loose rhetoric, into non-democratic roil to best, be bested;
weiring, weired we say,
  'No longer!' jolly fools about us will stroll!
 And we'll meet then, cloaked with fine beards, on the level field of Justice.

Notes: Pentheraphobe: fleer, fearer of pain, distress. Fair ancients: Plato. À la Buisson! To
the bushes. Vorfreude: Joy felt when thinking of good things (that will happen). Watts: Alan
Watts. Vates: [L.] prophet; soothsayer; poet. Chast: for chastise. Weiring: A weir - a net, as
if, to catch fish, or just net. A weiring to me: a feelers', in-touchers', Intuitionists' method,
specific or way. Wind weirs, the sun. Trees weir, and what's a spider doing, or a man or
woman building a house?

THOUGHT

If the chambered, meditative, said there is a stillness in thought
whose emotion has keyed the lock;
that efficiently, a stream exists there if energy
and quiet - very team of that force's churning flares;
  we welcome the light and keep the metaphysic.

 'No sight,' quoth Pound, 'is worth the beauty of my thought'
and of long held discoveries' old satisfactions told.
If Kant's critique of intuition being (pre)-thought and only source,
(or Martin H.'s speculative.) suffering 'professional' obscurity from the start
Mathematicians (cheer as ratio, the rational, demonstrable
take the sidelines, not blocking 'What ifs'), and some philosophers' gripes,
had not been ignored or worse, may have made compel
on man's before-thought blind.
    Though going before the self, in its darkness, is a troubled imagine.

 If at passages through life, anger blaring the quickest way to failure;
quicker by far than the attempt one had no heart for
 aligns for shoves at reason's disgrunt door; signal love, the
millennia of efforts' understandings, as grand protections there.

 If then, with these numbered and more assent,
ways along rough rock faces could open;
less competitions' false battlements - tries past goodness -
  man's paltry race might soften,
as faithed, but standard in its joy, the light (before aletheia)
always agrees, man has his, but life too has needs.

 Against these precipice, some probably properly cogged –
Body as carrier, Soul must spirit as passenger!
And 'scratching on folded tablets," continuing,
 as time rests less, shied of being finished, even hopeful Elysium.   183

Note: Much from our canceled philosopher of the last century – Martin H. "folded tablets": Iliad 6: 168-69.

END NOTE

The reader may notice a rather DIY look to the 'Contents,' and a couple of other pages. For instance as regards the two columns - Contents. Well, yes! They are just that. And I went as far as I was willing to make those Pages presentable.; the text being priority, which I pray comes through. I had no wonderful Bookbinder this time to design, layout and generally assist. Please find something of use in the foregoing. JMD!